EVOLVE

WORKBOOK

Samuela Eckstut

4

CAMBRIDGE
UNIVERSITY PRESS

Shaftesbury Road, Cambridge CB2 8EA, United Kingdom

One Liberty Plaza, 20th Floor, New York, NY 10006, USA

477 Williamstown Road, Port Melbourne, VIC 3207, Australia

314–321, 3rd Floor, Plot 3, Splendor Forum, Jasola District Centre, New Delhi – 110025, India

103 Penang Road, #05–06/07, Visioncrest Commercial, Singapore 238467

Cambridge University Press & Assessment is a department of the University of Cambridge.

We share the University's mission to contribute to society through the pursuit of education, learning and research at the highest international levels of excellence.

www.cambridge.org
Information on this title: www.cambridge.org/9781108409018

First published 2019

20 19 18 17 16 15 14 13 12 11 10 9

Printed in Malaysia by Vivar Printing

A catalogue record for this publication is available from the British Library

ISBN	978-1-108-40531-7	Student's Book
ISBN	978-1-108-40509-6	Student's Book A
ISBN	978-1-108-40923-0	Student's Book B
ISBN	978-1-108-40532-4	Student's Book with Practice Extra
ISBN	978-1-108-40510-2	Student's Book with Practice Extra A
ISBN	978-1-108-40925-4	Student's Book with Practice Extra B
ISBN	978-1-108-40901-8	Workbook with Audio
ISBN	978-1-108-40874-5	Workbook with Audio A
ISBN	978-1-108-41194-3	Workbook with Audio B
ISBN	978-1-108-40518-8	Teacher's Edition with Test Generator
ISBN	978-1-108-41071-7	Presentation Plus
ISBN	978-1-108-41204-9	Class Audio CDs
ISBN	978-1-108-40795-3	Video Resource Book with DVD
ISBN	978-1-108-41449-4	Full Contact with DVD
ISBN	978-1-108-41155-4	Full Contact A with DVD
ISBN	978-1-108-41417-3	Full Contact B with DVD

Additional resources for this publication at www.cambridge.org/evolve

Cambridge University Press & Assessment has no responsibility for the persistence or accuracy of URLs for external or third-party internet websites referred to in this publication, and does not guarantee that any content on such websites is, or will remain, accurate or appropriate. Information regarding prices, travel timetables, and other factual information given in this work is correct at the time of first printing but Cambridge University Press & Assessment does not guarantee the accuracy of such information thereafter.

CONTENTS

1 VOCABULARY: Describing accomplishments

A Circle the words to complete the phrase. One phrase has two correct answers.

1 break *a fear* / *a record*
2 face *a fear* / *a medal*
3 get *a business* / *a lot of likes*
4 have *a good joke* / *a sense of humor*
5 rise *to a challenge* / *a goal for myself*
6 run *a business* / *a marathon*
7 set *a goal for myself* / *pride in something*
8 take *a medal for something* / *pride in something*
9 tell *a goal for myself* / *a good joke*
10 win *a medal* / *a record*
11 work *with my hands* / *a business*

B Complete the sentences with phrases from exercise 1A.

1 When you _____run a business_____, you organize or control a business.
2 When you _____, you say something to make people laugh.
3 When you _____, you create something for your job.
4 When you _____, you get a prize in a competition.
5 When you post something online that many people think is good, you _____.
6 When you _____, you feel good about something you have done.
7 When you _____, you deal with something you are afraid of.
8 When you _____, you deal with a difficult job or opportunity successfully.
9 When you _____, you are involved in a really long race.
10 When you _____, you do something faster or better than anyone else.
11 When you _____, you decide something you want to do in the future.
12 When you _____, you are able to understand funny things and to be funny yourself.

C Imagine you are in these situations. What might you say? Use the phrases from exercise 1A to write a sentence for each.

1 **at a party:** _____Miranda, tell us a good joke._____
2 **at a job interview:** _____
3 **at a sporting event:** _____

2 GRAMMAR: Tense review (simple and continuous)

A **Some of the underlined verbs are not correct. Fix the mistakes.**

1 I ~~was going~~ *went* to a party last night. It <u>was</u> fun.

2 What <u>do</u> you <u>do</u> right now? <u>Are</u> you busy?

3 Jorge <u>has gotten</u> a job, but Rosa <u>has looked</u> for six months and <u>is</u> still <u>looking</u>.

4 <u>Have</u> you <u>heard</u> the news? Tony and Ana <u>have been getting</u> married.

5 I <u>talked</u> to Julia when you <u>called</u>. She <u>was telling</u> me a funny story.

B **Complete the paragraph with the correct form of the verbs in the box.**
Some verbs will be used more than once.

~~be~~	get	(not) see	take	talk	wait	walk

There ¹ _____*have been*_____ strange events in my neighborhood recently. I ² _____ down the street a couple of days ago when I ³ _____ a cow. Yes, that's right, a cow! You ⁴ _____ often _____ cows in the middle of a city. In fact, I ⁵ _____ never _____ one. But last Monday at 4:15 in the afternoon, there ⁶ _____ a cow in the middle of the road. Drivers ⁷ _____ out of their cars. A lot of people ⁸ _____ pictures. People in the neighborhood ⁹ _____ to each other about the cow ever since. We ¹⁰ _____ to see what the next strange event will be.

C **Write true sentences about you. Replace X with a word or phrase to complete each sentence.**

1 In my entire life, I / never / see / X

    In my entire life, I've never seen a cow on a street.

2 I / walk / down the street the other day when / X

    _____

3 You / often / (not) see / X / in my neighborhood

    _____

4 Once / I / X / but / I / never / X / it again

    _____

5 I / X / right now because I / X

    _____

6 I / try to / X / for a long time / but / I / still / X

    _____

1.2 THE RIGHT CANDIDATE

1 VOCABULARY: Describing key qualities

A Check (✓) the correct underlined words. Correct the incorrect words.

responsible
1 He is a very ~~responsibility~~ person. ☐
2 She has the right <u>qualifications</u> for the job. ☑
3 He has a lot of <u>curious</u>. ☐
4 I hope to be very <u>success</u> in the future. ☐
5 I like their <u>independence</u>. ☐
6 You're not very <u>ambitious</u>, are you? ☐
7 I'm very <u>experience</u>. ☐
8 It's important to treat people <u>polite</u>. ☐
9 This job requires a lot of <u>creativity</u>. ☐
10 She doesn't have much <u>enthusiastic</u>. ☐
11 Thank you for your <u>truthfulness</u>. ☐
12 Are you <u>confident</u> when you speak English? ☐

2 GRAMMAR: Stative and dynamic verbs

A Write *S* (stative verb) or *D* (dynamic verb).
1 Are you being truthful? D
2 We usually interview five people for every job. _____
3 I take a photography class on Tuesday evenings. _____
4 The report is very interesting. _____
5 Do you know Lily? _____
6 Why do they hate their job? _____
7 I need some help. _____
8 I'm thinking of changing jobs. _____

4

B   Complete each pair of sentences with the stative and dynamic use of the verb in parentheses ( ).

1   (see)   a   Tom _____ is seeing _____ the doctor. He'll be home soon.

   b   I _____ see _____ two people outside.

2   (have)   a   Melina _____ experience.

   b   The doctor's in the cafeteria. She _____ lunch.

3   (think)   a   We _____ about moving to a bigger place.

   b   What _____ you _____ of the class?

4   (smell)   a   He _____ the fish. Maybe there's something wrong with it.

   b   Everything _____ delicious. Let's eat!

5   (weigh)   a   The suitcase _____ 22 kilos.

   b   I don't know the price yet. The man _____ the meat now.

3   GRAMMAR AND VOCABULARY

A   Complete the job reference for Alex Martinez. Use the correct form of the verbs in parentheses ( ). What qualities from exercise 1A does he have? Circle them.

I ^{1} _____ know _____ (know) Alex well. I ^{2} _____ (know) him for ten years. He ^{3} _____ (work) at the company for six. He is a responsible person and ^{4} _____ (take) his job very seriously. He is definitely qualified for the job. He ^{5} _____ (have) two degrees and many years of experience. He's ambitious and clearly ^{6} _____ (want) to be successful. He ^{7} _____ (set) goals for himself and then ^{8} _____ (do) the work to achieve them. He is curious and loves to learn new things. He ^{9} _____ (talk) to a lot of people who are different from him and ^{10} _____ (try) to learn from them. In fact, right now he ^{11} _____ (take) two classes at the local community college in different subjects. I'm not surprised that Alex ^{12} _____ (look) for a job with more responsibilities. His confidence is just another one of his excellent qualities. We will be sorry to lose him.

B   Use the word prompts to write part of a job reference for someone you know. Replace X with a word or phrase to complete each sentence.

1   She/He / work / at this job / X years

   She has worked at this job for three years.

2   She/He / X / worker

   _____

   _____

3   Right now / she/he / X

   _____

   _____

4   Her/His / X / one of her/his excellent qualities

   _____

   _____

1.3 WE GO WAY BACK

1 FUNCTIONAL LANGUAGE: Making and responding to introductions

A **Complete the sentences. Match 1–7 in column A with a–g in column B.**

A

1 Do you …   _c_
2 I don't think …   _____
3 You're new …   _____
4 Do you two know …   _____
5 Have you …   _____
6 Let me introduce you …   _____
7 Is this your …   _____

B

a here, right?
b met my assistant?
c know anyone here?
d first day?
e to a couple of people.
f we've met before.
g each other?

B **Put the conversation in the correct order.**

Jack	Yes, I just started this morning.	_____
Jack	It's nice to meet you, Sofia.	_____
Sofia	Hello. I don't think we've met before.	_1_
Sofia	My name is Sofia.	_____
Sofia	It's nice to meet you, too. Is this your first day?	_____
Jack	No, we haven't met yet. I'm Jack.	_____

2 REAL-WORLD STRATEGY: Responding to an introduction

A **Complete the conversations. Use the words in the box.**

go   going   haven't   hi   I'm   love   met   see   ~~sure~~   went

1 **Dan** Have you met Sandra?
   Luis I'm not ____sure____ , but _____ , I'm Luis.
2 **Dan** Do you know Sandra?
   Chris Yes, we _____ way back. We _____ to school together. How's it _____ , Sandra?
3 **Dan** Have you met Sandra?
   Marta No, I _____ , but I'd _____ to. Hi, Sandra. _____ Marta.
4 **Dan** Do you two know each other?
   Ruta Yes, we _____ this morning! Nice to _____ you again, Sandra.

3 FUNCTIONAL LANGUAGE AND REAL-WORLD STRATEGY

A **Complete the conversation. Use the language you practiced in exercises 1A and 2A.**

1 Armando Hi. I don't think we've met before.
___You're new___ here, right?

Clara _____ yesterday

Armando I'm Armando.

Clara Nice _____. I'm Clara.

Armando Nice to meet you, too, Clara. Let me
_____. Tom, this is Clara.

Tom Hey Clara! _____?

Armando _____ each other?

Clara Yeah, _____ yesterday.

2 Sara Is this your _____?
I'm Sara.

Rick Hi Sara. It's _____.
I'm Rick.

Sara Do you _____?

Rick No, not yet.

Sara _____
to a couple of people. Zack, this is Rick.

Zack _____, Rick.

Rick _____, too.

B **Choose one of the following situations. Write a conversation introducing the people. Use the language you practiced in exercises 1 A and 2A.**

Situation 1: Marcel has just moved into your neighborhood. Introduce yourself.

Situation 2: Francesca is new to your class. Introduce her to some of your classmates.

A _____

B _____

A _____

B _____

1.4 FLIPPING YOUR JOB INTERVIEW

1 READING

A **Read the blog post. Then check (✓) the best title.**

1 Preparing for an interview? ☐

2 Getting the job you want! ☐

3 Dress for success! ☐

● ● ● ◄ ►   🔍 🏠

| **Blog** | **Share** | **Comment** |

You've finally gotten the interview you've wanted for months. Now you're busy preparing for the interview. You've researched the company and thought about the questions you want to ask.

What else is there? What you're going to wear. The way you look is very important. At the end of the interview, you want people to be talking about your experience, not your appearance.

What should you wear? Suits and ties for guys, and dresses for women? That's not always necessary. It depends on the type of job you're applying for.

Is it a job in the computer industry? You might not need a suit or a dress, but that doesn't mean you can go in a T-shirt and jeans. You need to look like you're going to work, not out for the night with friends. So, guys, put on a nice shirt and stylish pants. And, women, a nice sweater or blouse with a skirt or pants will be fine.

If you're interviewing for a finance job, you need to wear what people in the business world wear. That means a suit and tie for men and dresses or suits for women.

Dress for the job you want. Make sure your clothes are clean and ironed. Avoid wearing perfume or cologne, and don't wear too much makeup or jewelry.

Remember: If after the interview people are talking about your appearance, you probably won't hear from them again. So dress right and look good. Your career may depend on it.

B **READ FOR GIST** **Complete the statements. Use the phrases in the box.**

goes to a lot of job interviews	has interviewed people	buy clothes
is going to go to a job interview	get a job	interview people

1 The person who wrote the article is someone who _____ .

2 The person who reads the article is someone who _____ .

3 The purpose of the article is to help someone _____ .

2 LISTENING

A 🔊 **1.01** **Listen to the conversation. Answer the questions.**

1 When is the man's interview? _____

2 Where has he applied for a job? _____

3 What should he wear? _____

4 What's the problem? _____

3 WRITING

A Read the comments in response to the blog post in exercise 1A. Underline the sentence that shows agreement. Circle the sentence that shows disagreement. Put a box around the sentences that show appreciation.

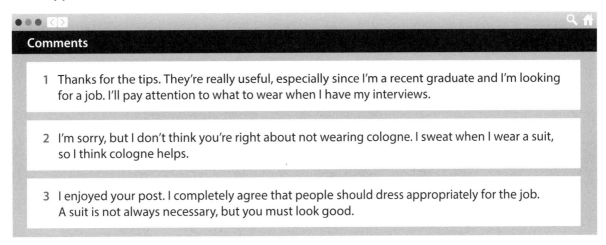

Comments

1 Thanks for the tips. They're really useful, especially since I'm a recent graduate and I'm looking for a job. I'll pay attention to what to wear when I have my interviews.

2 I'm sorry, but I don't think you're right about not wearing cologne. I sweat when I wear a suit, so I think cologne helps.

3 I enjoyed your post. I completely agree that people should dress appropriately for the job. A suit is not always necessary, but you must look good.

B Write two comments in response to the blog post in exercise 1A. In one comment, show appreciation and agree. In the second comment, disagree. Which comment reflects your true opinion?

CHECK AND REVIEW

Read the statements. Can you do these things?

UNIT 1	Mark the boxes. ☑ I can do it. ？ I am not sure. I can …		If you are not sure, go back to these pages in the Student's Book.
VOCABULARY	☐	use expressions to talk about personal achievements.	page 2
	☐	use nouns and adjectives to talk about key qualities employers look for.	page 4
GRAMMAR	☐	use a variety of simple and continuous verb forms.	page 3
	☐	use dynamic and stative verbs to talk about actions, habits, and states.	page 5
FUNCTIONAL LANGUAGE	☐	make introductions.	page 6
	☐	respond to an introduction.	page 7
SKILLS	☐	write a comment in response to a blog post.	page 9
	☐	agree, disagree, and show appreciation.	page 9

1 VOCABULARY: Describing trends

A Cross out the phrase that is different in meaning.

1	be a fad	be all the rage	~~be on the way out~~
2	be dated	be fashionable	be old-fashioned
3	come back in style	go out of fashion	lose popularity
4	be trendy	lose interest	gain popularity
5	be the next big thing	gain interest	go out of style
6	be on the way out	be the latest thing	be the next big thing

B Answer the questions about trends.

1 What is something you think is a fad?

In my opinion, long beards are a fad. I don't think they'll be popular next year.

2 What is a type of clothing you think is dated?

_____

3 What is a type of music that is gaining popularity?

_____

4 What is a type of music that is going out of style?

_____

5 What type of diets are trendy right now?

_____

6 What do you think will be the next big thing in fashion?

_____

7 What is something that is all the rage right now?

_____

8 What is something you think is old-fashioned?

_____

2 GRAMMAR: Real conditionals

A Put the words in the correct order to make sentences.

1 the server / to waste / want / for a doggy bag / ask / don't / you / the food / if

If you don't want to waste the food, ask the server for a doggy bag. OR Ask the server for a doggy bag if you don't want to waste the food.

2 people won't / just a fad / for very long / if / do / it's / it

3 the chocolate pizza / like / if / have / you / to try / different kinds of food / you

4 to waste food / if / get worse / the problem / continue / will / we

5 on social media / everyone / something / trending / pays attention / if / is

6 expensive / a restaurant / if / it / gourmet food / usually / is / serves

B Complete the sentences. Use the words in parentheses ( ).

1 Fish _____is_____ (be) good for you if it _____isn't_____ (not / be) fried.

2 If we _____ (not / put) the meat in the fridge soon, it _____ (go) bad.

3 If you _____ (be) allergic to nuts, _____ (not / eat) the cake. It has nuts.

4 _____ (not / drink) coffee at night if you _____ (have) trouble falling asleep.

5 If you _____ (make) dinner tomorrow, I _____ (cook) it tonight.

6 _____ (not / go) to Heaven Gourmet if you _____ (want) a cheap meal. It's an expensive place.

C How can people waste less food, eat better, and save money? Write your ideas. Use *if*.

If you don't eat a lot of fast food, you'll have a healthier diet.

FOOD YOU FERMENT

1 VOCABULARY: Preparing food

A **Cross out the food that is in a different food group.**

1 ~~pineapple~~   garlic   mint
2 eggplant   tuna   zucchini
3 garlic   shrimp   tuna
4 cabbage   pineapple   zucchini
5 ginger   mint   zucchini

B **Complete the sentences with words from exercise 1A. More than one answer may be possible.**

1 Mariel likes to put a little bit of _____ in her tea.

2 Do you have a stick of gum or a breath mint? The pasta I had for lunch had too much _____ in it.

3 Jack went fishing last weekend and caught a 40-lb _____!

4 I have to remove the shells from these _____ before we cook them. Can you help me?

5 _____ is probably my favorite vegetable. I just love its purple color.

C **Complete the sentences. Use the words in the box.**

~~barbecue~~	boil	chop	fry	rinse	stir

1 If you ____barbecue____ a steak, you usually do it outside.

2 If you _____ fruit, you usually do it at the sink.

3 You need a spoon to _____ something.

4 If you _____ water, it becomes very hot.

5 You need a knife to _____ something.

6 You need oil to _____ something.

D **Answer the questions with your own information.**

1 Which foods in exercise 1A do you like?

_____

2 Are there foods in exercise 1A you have never tried?

_____

3 How often do you use the cooking methods in exercise 1C?

_____

4 What dish do you eat that uses a food from exercise 1A and a cooking method from exercise 1C?

_____

2 GRAMMAR: Clauses with *when, until, after*

A **Underline the event in each sentence that happens first.**

1 The sauce will change color when <u>you add the garlic</u>.

2 As soon as the food is done, we'll eat.

3 Before the water boils, put in the cabbage.

4 Add the zucchini after you fry the fish.

5 Cook the rice until there's no more water in the pot.

6 Once we finish lunch, we'll wash the dishes.

B **Combine the sentences. Use the time expression in parentheses ( ).**

1 I'm going to reserve a table. Then I'll tell you the time. (after)

   After I reserve a table, I'll tell you the time. OR *I'll tell you the time after I reserve a table.*

2 We'll get to the restaurant. Then we'll text you. (when)

3 We'll wait outside. You will arrive. (until)

4 The server will give us the menu. We'll order. (as soon as)

5 We'll pay the bill. Then we'll leave. (once)

6 We'll have dinner. Then we'll go to the movies. (before)

C **Write the correct form of the verb in parentheses ( ).**
   Then complete the sentence with your own information.

1 When I _____*cook*_____ (cook) a big meal, _____*I'll invite all my friends*_____ .

2 After I _____ (get up) tomorrow morning, _____ .

3 I _____ (not go) to bed until _____ .

4 As soon as I _____ (have) some free time, _____ .

5 Once I _____ (save) enough money, _____ .

1   FUNCTIONAL LANGUAGE: Make, accept, and refuse offers

A   **Change the underlined words in the sentences without changing the meaning. Use the words in the box.**

| I'm OK | ~~a refill~~ | care for | get | here |
| Awesome | offer | Oh | wonderful | want |

                    a refill

1 A   Can I get you ~~another juice~~?

   B   <u>I'd better not</u>, thanks.

2 A   Would you <u>like</u> some juice?

   B   That'd be <u>great</u>.

3 A   Can I <u>get</u> you another dessert?

   B   <u>Yes</u>, that's great.

4 A   Can I <u>have</u> another sausage, please?

   B   Sure, <u>there</u> you go.

5 A   Anyone else <u>care for</u> some cake? We have three different kinds.

   B   <u>That's great</u>, I'll check it out.

2   REAL-WORLD STRATEGY: Acknowledge an acceptance

A   **Read each conversation. Use the words below to complete each response.**

| back | got | right | sure |

1 A   Can I offer you anything to drink?

   B   Yes. Some coffee would be great.

   A   I'll be right _____ with that.

2 A   Would you pass me another cookie, please?

   B   _____ thing.

3 A   Is there any more iced tea?

   B   Coming _____ up!

4 A   Could I have a little more cake? It's delicious.

   B   You _____ it!

B   **Write two conversations. Speaker A makes an offer of food or drink. Speaker B accepts or refuses.**

1 A _____

   B _____

   A _____

2 A _____

   B _____

   A _____

3 FUNCTIONAL LANGUAGE AND REAL-WORLD STRATEGY

A What do people often offer in these situations? Write three things.

On an airplane	At a party	At a business meeting	At a restaurant
something to drink			
a snack			
a blanket			

B Write conversations for each remaining situation in exercise 3A. Have people accept and refuse the offers.

Flight attendant	Would you like something to drink?
Passenger	Yes, I'd love a glass of water.
Flight attendant	Coming right up!

Flight attendant	Can I get you a snack?
Passenger	I'd better not, thanks.

Flight attendant	Would you care for a blanket?
Passenger	That'd be wonderful.

Conversation 1

A _____

B _____

A _____

B _____

A _____

B _____

A _____

Conversation 2

A _____

B _____

A _____

B _____

A _____

B _____

A _____

Conversation 3

A _____

B _____

A _____

B _____

A _____

B _____

A _____

1 LISTENING

A   🔊 **2.01** **LISTEN FOR GIST** **Listen to a conversation between a man and a woman. Where do they decide to have lunch? Why?**

B   🔊 **2.01** **Listen again. Read the statements. Write *T* (true) or *F* (false). Correct the statements that are false.**

1   The woman is on a gluten-free diet because she wants to lose weight. _____

2   The woman has avoided eating things with gluten for the past six months. _____

3   The woman's family is also on a gluten-free diet. _____

4   The man and the woman are definitely going to lunch at Anna's. _____

2 READING

A   **Read about the results of a survey about gluten-free diets. Circle the questions that the survey asked. Answer the questions you circle.**

> Gluten-free diets seem all the rage nowadays. You can see gluten-free foods in supermarkets and restaurants. News about the gluten-free diets of movie stars and professional athletes is all over social media. But what do people really know about gluten-free foods? Our survey results have some surprises.
>
> A majority of the people who responded said that being on a gluten-free diet improves physical or mental health. About 22 percent said they buy gluten-free products or try to avoid gluten.
>
> A quarter of the people in the survey thought that gluten-free foods have more nutrients than food with gluten. The truth is just the opposite.
>
> More than a third of the people interviewed thought that a gluten-free diet will help them lose weight. However, there is no research that proves this to be true. In fact, studies have shown that gluten-free diets can increase the risk of becoming overweight.

1   Does being on a gluten-free diet improve physical or mental health?

_____

2   Do you buy gluten-free products or try to avoid gluten?

_____

3   Is gluten-free food less expensive?

_____

4   Do gluten-free foods have more nutrients than food with gluten?

_____

5   Will a gluten-free diet help you lose weight?

_____

3 WRITING

A   Look at the charts from a college survey on what students drink. What trends do they show?

**Students who drink soda vs.
sugar-free drinks – 2010**

- 60% of students drink soda
- 40% drink sugar-free drinks

**Students who drink soda vs.
sugar-free drinks – 2015**

- 40% of students drink soda
- 60% drink sugar-free drinks

B   Write a short report about the survey results. You can use the phrases below. Make sure you include numbers from the chart.

gain/lose popularity be the next big thing	be trendy	be on the way out	be a thing of the past

CHECK AND REVIEW

Read the statements. Can you do these things?

UNIT 2	Mark the boxes. ✔ I can do it. ? I am not sure. I can …	If you are not sure, go back to these pages in the Student's Book.
VOCABULARY	☐ use expressions to describe trends.	page 12
	☐ use the correct words to describe food preparation.	page 14
GRAMMAR	☐ use real conditionals.	page 13
	☐ refer to the future with time clauses using *when*, *until*, and *after*.	page 15
FUNCTIONAL LANGUAGE	☐ make, accept, and refuse offers.	page 16
	☐ acknowledge an acceptance	page 17
SKILLS	☐ write survey results.	page 19
	☐ reference numbers and statistics.	page 19

1 VOCABULARY: Talking about time and money

A Circle the correct words to complete the sentences.

1 If you <u>can't afford</u> to do something, you don't have the *time /(money)*.

2 If you have a good work-life <u>balance</u>, the amount of time you spend at work and doing things you enjoy are *about the same / very different*.

3 When you <u>boost</u> your chances of getting a job, you *decrease / increase* your chances.

4 The <u>cost of living</u> is the amount of money you need for *food, housing, and other basic things / parties, vacations, and other fun things*.

5 Your <u>lifestyle</u> is the *days of your life / way that you live*.

6 If you have a good <u>quality of life</u>, you have a lot of *money / satisfaction*.

7 Your <u>standard of living</u> is how much *money and comfort / money and family* you have.

8 If you <u>take a salary cut</u>, your salary goes *down / up*.

9 If something is <u>time well-spent</u>, it *takes a lot of time / is a good use of time*.

10 If you <u>trade</u> something, you *buy / exchange* it.

11 If you <u>value</u> something, it is *expensive / important to you*.

12 If something is <u>worth it</u>, it is difficult but *cheap / useful*.

B Complete the sentences with your own information.

1 I can't afford to _____ *move to a nicer place* _____ right now.

2 The thing I like most about my lifestyle is _____

_____ .

3 You know you don't have a good work-life balance when _____

_____ .

4 I would like to boost my chances of _____

_____ .

5 What I value most of all is _____

_____ .

6 It is time well-spent when I _____

_____ .

7 It's worth it to take a salary cut _____

_____ .

8 In order to have a good quality of life, it is important to _____

_____ .

GRAMMAR: *too* and *enough*

A   **Complete the sentences with *too* or *enough*. Use the words in the box.**

close	~~experienced~~	free time	money	slow	small

1   Jorge's too inexperienced for the job. He isn't _____experienced enough_____ .
2   The job is too far from my home. It isn't _____ .
3   Lina isn't quick enough. She's _____ .
4   I work too many hours. I don't have _____ .
5   My salary is too low. I don't make _____ .
6   The office isn't big enough. It's _____ .

B   **Write sentences. Use the words in parentheses ( ) with *(not) too, too much, too many,* or *enough,* and the infinitive.**

1   I want to go to the beach, but it's only 63° outside. (cold)
    It's too cold to go to the beach.
2   Ramón can't go to the club. He isn't 21 yet. (old)
    _____
3   Olga is tired after work, but she still cooks dinner. (tired)
    _____
4   Isabelle wants to take a long vacation, but she has only five vacation days. (time off)
    _____
5   Manuel can't go out for lunch. He's finishing a report. (busy)
    _____
6   It costs $20 to enter the museum. Trevor only has $15. (money)
    _____

C   **Write sentences that are true for you. Use *enough, too, too much,* or *too many.***

1   I / spend / time studying
    I spend too much time studying. OR _I don't spend enough time studying._
2   I / have / things to do today
    _____
3   I / make / money
    _____
4   I / get / texts every day
    _____
5   My neighborhood / be / lively / at night
    _____
6   I / have / friends on social media
    _____
7   I / work / hard
    _____

3.2 THE PRICE OF A COFFEE

1 VOCABULARY: Talking about prices and value

A **Complete the chart. Write each verb under the correct preposition.**

charge	come up	depend	have an effect
invest	rely	make the most	pay a fair price
play an important role	suggest a price	take advantage	treat myself

for	on	of
charge		

in	to	with

B **Complete the sentences with the verbs and prepositions in exercise 1A.**

1 You should _____make the most of_____ the beautiful weather today. It's going to rain tomorrow.

2 Prices _____ what people are willing to pay.

3 Drinking too much coffee _____ my ability to sleep at night.

4 After a bad day, I _____ a bowl of ice cream.

5 Our guests can _____ many facilities at the hotel, such as restaurants, meeting rooms, and workout rooms.

6 I am willing to _____ food, but I think $12 for a sandwich is too much.

7 You can _____ the service at the restaurant. It's always fast.

8 To be successful, businesses need to _____ new ideas on a regular basis.

9 Should I _____ Sam's business? I'll make money if it's successful.

10 I'll never go back to that restaurant. They _____ a glass of water!

C **Use at least three of the phrases in exercise 1A to write about shopping.**

The last time I went shopping, the cashier forgot to charge me
for two things.

_____

_____

_____

_____

_____

_____

_____

GRAMMAR: Modifying comparisons

A Compare the bakeries below. Use the words in parentheses ( ) and *a bit, a little, much, a lot, more,* *way more,* or *by far.*

	Bob's Bakery	Crazy 4 Cake	Sweet Surprises
Price for cakes	$15	$25	$12
Busy times	11 a.m.–3 p.m.	all day	12 p.m.–2 p.m.
Likes	255	765	450
In business since	1952	2008	2010

1 Crazy 4 Cake has been open _____ *a little longer* _____ than Sweet
   Surprises. Of the three, Bob's Bakery has been open
   _____ . (long)

2 Crazy 4 Cake is _____ , but Bob's Bakery is
   _____ than Sweet Surprises. (expensive)

3 Sweet Surprises is _____ than Bob's Bakery,
   but Crazy 4 Cake is _____ . (popular)

4 Crazy 4 Cake is _____ of the three. Bob's Bakery
   is _____ than Sweet Surprises. (busy)

B Complete the sentences with *as … as* and *almost, nearly,* *nowhere near,* or *just.*

1 The pizza at Arturo's is much better than the pizza at Gina's.
   Gina's pizza is _____ *not nearly as good as* _____ Arturo's.

2 The servers at Gina's are a little friendlier than the servers at
   Arturo's.
   Arturo's servers are _____ Gina's are.

3 The seats at Gina's are really comfortable. Arturo's seats aren't comfortable at all.
   Arturo's seats are _____ Gina's are.

4 Arturo's and Gina's are big. They both have 25 tables.
   Gina's is _____ Arturo's is.

5 Gina's and Arturo's are new. Gina's opened in June of 2017. Arturo's opened six months later.
   Gina's is _____ Arturo's is.

C Write true sentences about yourself. Replace X and Y with a word or phrase to complete each sentence.

1 X / by far / exciting / thing / I've ever seen.
   The circus is by far the most exciting thing I've ever seen.

2 X / by far / good / gift / I've ever gotten.
   _____

3 X / nowhere near / tasty / Y
   _____

4 X / way / easy / Y
   _____

5 X / a bit / expensive / Y
   _____

6 X / just / intelligent / Y
   _____

3.3 I'M SO SORRY!

1 FUNCTIONAL LANGUAGE: Apologize for damaging something

A **Complete the conversation. Use the words in the box.**

can't	didn't	don't	dumbest	how	so	~~sorry~~	what

Martin I'm really ¹____sorry____, but I just did the ²_____ thing.

Althea Oh no, ³_____ tell me something happened to my car. Did someone steal it?

Martin No, no. The car's outside. It's just that I had a small accident. You'll never guess ⁴_____ I did.

Althea What happened?

Martin I was parking the car and hit a tree. I can't tell you ⁵_____ sorry I am.

Althea A tree?

Martin I know. I ⁶_____ believe I ⁷_____ see it. I am ⁸_____ sorry. I'll pay for the damage.

Althea Let me call the insurance company and see if they'll pay. But first, let me see the car.

2 REAL-WORLD STRATEGY: Responding to an apology

A **Respond to the apologies. Put the words in the correct order.**

1 **Glen** I'm so sorry I was late for the meeting.
   Andy deal / it's / big / really / no

   _____

   _____

2 **Delcy** I can't believe I forgot your birthday.
   Nate over / don't / yourself / it / beat / up

   _____

   _____

3 **Ron** I'm really sorry I didn't pick you up on time.
   Hee-an end / the / the / not / world / it's / of

   _____

   _____

FUNCTIONAL LANGUAGE AND REAL-WORLD STRATEGY

A **Write a conversation for each situation. Use the language you practiced in exercises 1A and 2A.**

1 Victor lost Daria's book. He left it on the train. Daria doesn't want him to feel bad about it.

Victor   *Daria, I can't believe I did this but …*

Daria   *Oh no, what?*

Victor   *I left your book on the train. I can't tell you how sorry I am.*

Daria   *It's just a book. Don't beat yourself up over it.*

2 Keiko forgot about a meeting. She didn't put it on her calendar. Al doesn't want her to feel bad about it.

Keiko

Al

Keiko

Al

3 Joao texted Max the wrong directions, and Max got lost. Max doesn't want him to feel bad about it.

Joao

Max

Joao

Max

4 Alex is out of town. His friend Lin is staying at his apartment. Lin calls Alex to tell him something has happened and to apologize. Alex thinks Lin is going to tell him he broke the TV.

Lin

Alex

Lin

Alex

5 Hector says he broke one of Alice's good glasses. Alice doesn't want him to feel bad about it.

Hector

Alice

Hector

Alice

3.4 EPIC SHOPPING FAILS

1 READING

A **Read the blog post about shopping. Is the blogger writing about shopping online or in a store?**

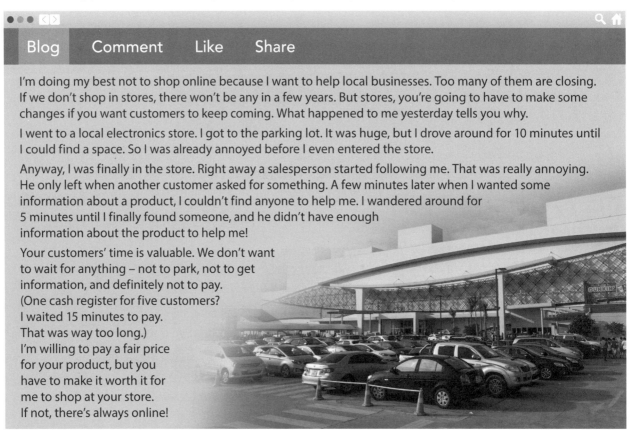

Blog | Comment | Like | Share

I'm doing my best not to shop online because I want to help local businesses. Too many of them are closing. If we don't shop in stores, there won't be any in a few years. But stores, you're going to have to make some changes if you want customers to keep coming. What happened to me yesterday tells you why.

I went to a local electronics store. I got to the parking lot. It was huge, but I drove around for 10 minutes until I could find a space. So I was already annoyed before I even entered the store.

Anyway, I was finally in the store. Right away a salesperson started following me. That was really annoying. He only left when another customer asked for something. A few minutes later when I wanted some information about a product, I couldn't find anyone to help me. I wandered around for 5 minutes until I finally found someone, and he didn't have enough information about the product to help me!

Your customers' time is valuable. We don't want to wait for anything – not to park, not to get information, and definitely not to pay. (One cash register for five customers? I waited 15 minutes to pay. That was way too long.) I'm willing to pay a fair price for your product, but you have to make it worth it for me to shop at your store. If not, there's always online!

B **READ FOR DETAIL** **Read the post again. Answer the questions.**

1 What does the blogger say about the parking lot?

   a It was too small. b It was too full.

2 Why wasn't the salesperson helpful?

   a He didn't know about the product. b He was rude.

3 What other problem did the blogger have?

   a She had to wait too long to pay. b The store didn't have the product she wanted.

2 LISTENING

A 🔊 **3.01** **Listen to the conversation. Answer the questions.**

1 What kind of business does the woman work at? _____

2 Who gives her problems at work? _____

3 What did the Milk Lady do? _____

4 Why can't the woman fix the problem? _____

3 WRITING

A Read the store review. Underline the sentence that shows the reviewer's feeling. Circle the positive and negative features of the store. Put a box around the sentence that gives a recommendation.

● ● ● ◁ ▷   🔍 🏠

Store review

I highly recommend ProSports. I recently bought a tennis racket there. It's an excellent store with a wide variety of products and great prices. I couldn't find anything cheaper online. My only complaint is that there wasn't enough staff. Everyone was very friendly and knew a lot about the products, but there wasn't enough staff to take care of all the customers. Maybe that was because too many people know that ProSports is such a great store. It was my first time there. I'd definitely go back.

B Think of a store you have been to recently. Write a short review of the store.

_____

_____

_____

_____

_____

_____

_____

_____

CHECK AND REVIEW

Read the statements. Can you do these things?

UNIT 3	Mark the boxes. ✔ I can do it. ? I am not sure. I can …	If you are not sure, go back to these pages in the Student's Book.
VOCABULARY	☐ use expressions to talk about time and money. ☐ use verb phrases to talk about prices and value.	page 22 page 24
GRAMMAR	☐ use (not) too and (not) enough to talk about quantity. ☐ use modifiers in comparisons.	page 23 page 25
FUNCTIONAL LANGUAGE	☐ apologize for damaging something. ☐ respond to an apology.	page 26 page 27
SKILLS	☐ write a product review. ☐ describe feelings and give recommendations.	page 29 page 29

1   VOCABULARY: Talking about advertising

A   **Complete the sentences with words in the box.**

advertise	ad/advertisement	brands	commercials	fashion statement
logo	merchandise	merchandising	products	slogan
~~sponsor (n.)~~	sponsor (v.)	status symbols		

1   Al's Pizza pays to support our basketball team. They are our _____sponsor_____ . We have their _____ – "Best pizza in town!" – on our jerseys.

2   Louisa wears bright colors to make a _____ .

3   Dave's business was not doing well, so he decided to _____ on TV. He also hired an artist to design a new _____ for his business.

4   Have you seen the _____ for that new TV show? It looks really funny.

5   _____ from famous _____ , like Gucci and Prada, are often more expensive because they are _____ .

6   Disney makes a lot of its profits from _____ . The company charges other companies to put its characters on their products.

7   Many websites make money by hosting _____ for other companies and products.

8   Many companies will _____ a local charity or a sports team because they know it is good for their reputation.

9   The football stadium has a store inside that sells the team's _____ .

2   GRAMMAR: Modals of speculation

A   **Circle the correct words.**

1   The fans are going to their seats. They *can't* / *must* have tickets.

2   Val was in second place in the race last time. She *might* / *must* win this time.

3   Andreas always wears a Santos jersey. He *could* / *must* like the team.

4   There's a man talking to the players. He *must* / *could* be the coach. Or maybe he's the referee.

5   Some fans are leaving the game early. They *can't* / *might* be bored.

6   Nobody is wearing a jacket. It *can't* / *could* be cold.

B **Complete the conversations. Use *could*, *might*, *must*, or *can't* and the verb in parentheses ( ).**

1 **A** Does Victor know Eve?

   B He _____must know_____ (know) her. They're taking the same class.

2 **A** Are there tickets available for tomorrow's game?

   B There _____ (be) tickets left. Let's look online and see.

3 **A** That's Marisol's brother.

   B He _____ (be) Marisol's brother. Everyone in her family is tall, and he's very short.

4 **A** Does Natalia like soccer?

   B She _____ (like) it. She talks about it all the time.

5 **A** We have a meeting tomorrow, right?

   B We _____ (have) a meeting. Mark hasn't decided yet.

6 **A** Tom's at the door.

   B Tom _____ (be) at the door. He's at work.

3 GRAMMAR AND VOCABULARY

A **Write an explanation for each fact. Use modals of speculation and the words in the box or your own ideas.**

be rich	be well known	help people to remember
help to sell merchandise	~~look good~~	make (someone) feel special

1 Christine likes to make a fashion statement with her choice of clothes.

   It might be important for her to look good.

2 Nike has had the slogan "Just do it" for years.

   _____

   _____

3 People like to buy cool brands.

   _____

   _____

4 Commercials with music are more successful than commercials without music.

   _____

   _____

5 People buy Rolex watches because they are a status symbol.

   _____

   _____

6 A good logo is very important for a company.

   _____

   _____

VIRAL STORIES

1 VOCABULARY: Talking about people in the media

A **Look at the clues and complete the crossword.**

ACROSS

2 This person gets paid to wear the latest designs.

5 This word has a similar meaning to *performer*.

7 Beyonce is more than just a singer.
  She's a cultural …

8 This person plays music so people can dance.

9 This person is paid to tell jokes.

10 This is someone who is famous.

DOWN

1 This word has a similar meaning to *director*.

3 This is someone who is brave or who
  people admire.

4 This person makes new fashions.

6 At a concert, these are the people in
  the crowd.

2 GRAMMAR: Subject and object relative clauses

A **Write *where, which, who, that,* or – (if a relative pronoun is not necessary).**

1 I like stores __that__ OR __which__ have a lot of different products.

2 I never go to restaurants _____ I have to wait.

3 My friends _____ live far away text me all the time.

4 I share all the photos _____ I take with friends and family.

5 I don't like problems _____ keep me awake at night.

6 I don't give money to people _____ I don't know.

7 I would like to be someone _____ other people admire.

B   **Combine the sentences. Use relative pronouns where necessary.**
1   Some stories are unbelievable. The stories go viral.
    Some stories that go viral are unbelievable.
2   The stories are about animals. I like those stories the most.
    The stories that I like the most are about animals.
3   People must have a lot of free time. These people watch a lot of videos.

4   People share stories. They think the stories are funny.

5   There's a video with a cat. The cat is playing the piano.

6   Once I saw a video of a house. Fifty cats lived in the house.

7   One great video still makes me laugh. I saw the video last year.

8   My friends thought it was funny, too. My friends saw the video.

3   GRAMMAR AND VOCABULARY

A   **Write sentences that are true for you. Use relative pronouns where necessary.**
1   performers / perform online / always / get / a lot of likes
    Performers who perform online don't always get a lot of likes. OR *Performers who perform online always*
    get a lot of likes.
2   a podcaster / become / a celebrity / always / make / a lot of money

3   the icons / I / admire / be / all from my country

4   it / be / fun / to be in an audience / I / don't know anyone

5   the photos / go viral / be / always / photos of heroes

6   the clothes / I / buy / be / usually / by famous designers

4.3 | THAT'S A GOOD POINT, BUT ...

1 FUNCTIONAL LANGUAGE: Exchanging opinions

A **Match the columns to complete the conversations.**

1 I really think professional athletes are paid too much. _____

2 I find it very unfair that women athletes earn less than men. _____

3 I don't really think it's better to watch sports live than on TV. _____

4 High school students should focus on their studies, not on sports. _____

5 Don't you think we expect too much from professional athletes? _____

a As I see it, they have a responsibility to be good role models. _____

b Yes, absolutely. There's no reason they should earn less. _____

c It's not so much that it's better. It's just different. _____

d Just a second. Pro athletes train really hard. They earn their salaries. _____

e OK, that's a good point, but high school sports aren't all bad. _____

B **Complete the conversation with the expressions in the box.**

I really think	just a second	as I see it	that's a good point	I found it
it's just that	that's true but	it's not so much that		

Derek   So, Elisa, what did you think of the book?

Elisa   I hated it. ¹_____ really boring.

Derek   Yeah, me too. ²_____ it's the worst book we've read this year.

Tae-hyun   Now, ³_____. I liked it. It was so different from the stuff we usually read.

Elisa   ⁴_____, but being different doesn't mean it was good.

Tae-hyun   Well, Derek, I'm surprised you didn't like it. You usually love science fiction.

Derek   ⁵_____ this book was more about the relationship between the two main characters – not really about the space travel. ⁶_____, this book was really more of a love story.

Tae-hyun   ⁷_____ it's a love story, ⁸_____ love is an important part of the story. I still think it's science fiction.

2 REAL-WORLD STRATEGY: Making opinions more emphatic

A **Correct the mistakes in the responses.**

1 A The Aztecs are the best team in the league.

   B Sorry, I can't disagree more!

2 A Romantic comedies are always so dumb.

   B That's not true in all!

3 A Manu Ginobili wasn't that great of a basketball player.

   B You have it wrong!

3 FUNCTIONAL LANGUAGE AND REAL-WORLD STRATEGY

A **Read the conversation. Circle the expressions that discuss or exchange opinions. Underline the expressions that make opinions more emphatic.**

A What are you doing?

B Just reading one of those online gossip sites.

A Why do you read that trash?

B Now just a second, there's a lot of really good celebrity news here.

A As I see it, it's mostly just lies. Hardly any of that stuff is true.

B That's not true at all. When Khloe Kardashian had her baby, where do you think I read about it? On this site. That wasn't made up, was it?

A OK, that's true, but it's still just gossip. It's not news – it doesn't have any effect on your life.

B You have it all wrong. I don't read this site for news. I read it to be entertained. Not every news site has to be serious.

A It's not so much that I think all news has to be serious, it's just that I think the stories on this site are so dumb. I don't even find it entertaining.

B Well I couldn't disagree more. Now, if you don't mind, I going to finish reading this article.

B **Read Yusef's and Abigail's opinions on camping. Then write a conversation between Yusef and Abigail about camping. Use expressions to discuss and exchange opinions, and to make opinions more emphatic.**

Yusef	I love camping! I love getting out of the city and away from all the noise. It's just a lot of fun. You get to sleep outside and see the stars, cook over a fire, and maybe see some wildlife. It's really my favorite way to spend a weekend.

Abigail	Camping is the worst! You have to sleep outside, and there are bugs everywhere. And I'm constantly scared that I'll see a bear or some other wild animal. I guess cooking over a fire is OK, but I can barbeque in my backyard!

Yusef _____

Abigail _____

Yusef _____

Abigail _____

Yusef _____

Abigail _____

Yusef _____

Abigail _____

4.4 BUILDING A BRAND

1 LISTENING

A 🔊 **4.01** **LISTEN FOR GIST** Listen to the podcast. What does the speaker talk about?

B 🔊 **4.01** **LISTEN FOR DETAILS** Listen again. Answer the questions. Write *Y* (yes) or *N* (no).

1 Does the speaker say that every company can be successful internationally? _____

2 Should a company that does not have enough customers at home sell abroad? _____

3 Could a company fail abroad if it doesn't understand the culture of a country? _____

4 Is it important for companies to work with people from other countries? _____

2 READING

A **Read the article. Write the missing information.**

Red Bull is an example of an international success story. The brand has become so popular that people don't even realize where the drink comes from. They think it is either from their country or the United States. Very few people know that Red Bull is Austrian.

Actually, Red Bull is even more international. The owner, Dietrich Mateschitz, got the idea for Red Bull from an energy drink in Thailand. It was called Krating Daeng, which is Thai for "red bull." Dietrich Mateschitz discovered Krating Daeng during a trip to Asia in 1982. He went into business with Chaleo Yoovidhya, the creator of the Thai drink. Mateschitz made some changes to the flavor and started selling Red Bull in Austria in 1987.

Today Red Bull is sold around the world. It is not only a drink. With its slogan "Red Bull gives you wings," it has become a lifestyle icon.

1 Red Bull is an _____ company.

2 The name of the owner is _____.

3 The owner became interested in Red Bull when he was in _____.

4 *Krating Daeng* means _____.

5 Chaleo Yoovidhya was the person _____.

32

3 WRITING

A Read the social media comment. Underline the five words and phrases that mean "because (of)" and "so."

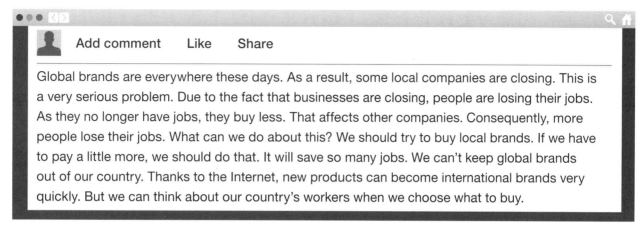

Add comment   Like   Share

Global brands are everywhere these days. As a result, some local companies are closing. This is a very serious problem. Due to the fact that businesses are closing, people are losing their jobs. As they no longer have jobs, they buy less. That affects other companies. Consequently, more people lose their jobs. What can we do about this? We should try to buy local brands. If we have to pay a little more, we should do that. It will save so many jobs. We can't keep global brands out of our country. Thanks to the Internet, new products can become international brands very quickly. But we can think about our country's workers when we choose what to buy.

B Write a comment about one of the topics in the box. Use at least three of the words or phrases you underlined in exercise 3A.

> your opinion about buying global brands   a brand you always buy
> a brand you used to like that no longer exists

_____

_____

_____

_____

_____

CHECK AND REVIEW

Read the statements. Can you do these things?

UNIT 4	Mark the boxes. ☑ I can do it. ? I am not sure. I can ...	If you are not sure, go back to these pages in the Student's Book.
VOCABULARY	☐ describe different features of ads and the techniques used.	page 34
	☐ talk about celebrities and viral news.	page 36
GRAMMAR	☐ make speculations.	page 35
	☐ use pronouns in relative clauses.	page 37
FUNCTIONAL LANGUAGE	☐ give, respond to, and critique opinions.	page 38
	☐ make opinions more emphatic.	page 39
SKILLS	☐ write a comment about local and global brands.	page 41
	☐ write about cause and effect.	page 41

1 VOCABULARY: Describing stories

A **Complete the sentences with words from the box. There may be more than one answer.**

~~family saga~~	horror story	personal tragedy
tall tale	feel-good story	human interest story
mystery	hard-luck story	love story
success story	tear jerker	

1 This kind of story is long and is about many different family members and events. _____family saga_____

2 In this kind of story, the main character faces death, injury, or great difficulties. _____

3 In this kind of story, we feel sorry for the problems someone has. _____

4 This kind of story is about two people who develop strong positive feelings for each other. _____

5 This kind of story is about someone who has a lot of achievements. _____

6 This kind of story is about something strange or unusual that happened. _____

7 In this kind of story, someone tells us something he or she says is true, but that is hard to believe. _____

8 This kind of story is intended to make us feel sorry for the person who tells the story. _____

9 This kind of story gives people happy feelings about life. _____

10 This kind of story surprises people and makes them afraid. _____

11 In this kind of story we connect emotionally with a person's problems, concerns or achievements. _____

2 GRAMMAR: Past perfect

A **Match sentences 1–6 with the sentences in the box. Then underline the events that happened first.**

~~I hadn't studied.~~	He'd missed his flight.	I had lost it.
He woke up in the hospital.	The party was over.	The movie had ended.

1 I failed the exam.   _I hadn't studied._

2 The money wasn't in my pocket. _____

3 He'd had an accident. _____

4 He arrived 10 minutes late. _____

5 I left the theater. _____

6 Everyone had left. _____

B   **Complete the paragraph below. Use the past perfect form of the words in the box.**

| be | ~~break~~ | open | put | take | throw |

Julio and Marcella came home late from a party one evening. They were shocked to see that one of the living room windows was broken. Someone [1] *had broken* the glass. The back door was unlocked. Someone [2] _____ the door. The dog was in the basement. Someone [3] _____ the dog there. They found their books and important papers on the floor. Someone [4] _____ them off the desk. Their laptops were gone. Someone [5] _____ them. Julio and Marcella called the police because they [6] _____ robbed.

3   GRAMMAR AND VOCABULARY

A   **Read the story below. Put the events in the correct order. Then decide: Is it a personal tragedy, a feel-good story, or a family saga?**

_____   His parents are very worried.

___1___   A young boy goes fishing with his dog.

_____   The boy is missing for 12 hours.

_____   After a few hours, the boy gets lost.

_____   The parents are very happy.

_____   Luckily, the dog helps him find his way home again.

B   **Complete the story from exercise 3A. Use the simple past, past continuous, and past perfect.**

A young boy had gone fishing with his dog. After a few hours, _____

_____

_____

_____

_____

_____

_____

_____

_____

5.2 LAST-MINUTE-ITIS

1 VOCABULARY: Making and breaking plans

A Complete the phrasal verbs with *ahead, down, out, forward,* or *together.*

Jess Hi, Leo. What happened last night? We all got ¹ ___together___ at the new pizza place in town. We thought you were coming but then we gave ² _____ on you.

Leo Yeah, I know. Sorry I let you ³ _____ . I don't mean to make ⁴ _____ excuses, but yesterday was just the worst day. First, my car was stolen. I ended ⁵ _____ taking three buses to Gina's place. Then she split ⁶ _____ with me.

Jess Really? I'm so sorry. That's terrible. A day like that could mess ⁷ _____ your whole month.

Leo Thanks Jess. Right now I'm just trying to stay positive. Anyway, I'm headed to lunch now. Should I wait for you or go ⁸ _____ without you?

Jess Don't wait. I'm going to be held ⁹ _____ here a little longer. Do you want to do something later today, maybe to cheer you ¹⁰ _____ ?

Leo Thanks, but tonight I'm going to hang ¹¹ _____ with my family. And I also feel like I'm getting a cold.

Jess Well, I'm sure you're looking ¹² _____ to your vacation at least. Vacations always make me feel better.

Leo Definitely. After all this it will be nice to get away for a couple of days. But let's get ¹³ _____ when I'm back.

2 GRAMMAR: *was/were going to*; *was/were supposed to*

A Check (✓) the correct sentences.

1 I was going call you, but I forgot. ☐

2 We were going to leave at 8, but we left at 9. ☑

3 The kids were suppose to get out of school an hour ago. Where are they? ☐

4 You going to pay me last week. I'm still waiting for the money. ☐

5 It supposed to rain today, but it's a beautiful day. ☐

6 Was I supposed to meet Professor Yu yesterday? I can't remember. ☐

B Now correct the incorrect sentences from exercise 2A.

I was going to call you, but I forgot.

_____

_____

_____

_____

C   **Manuel checked the things he did last week. Complete the sentences about the things he did <u>not</u> do. Use *was/were going to* in 1–3 and *was/were supposed to* in 4–6.**

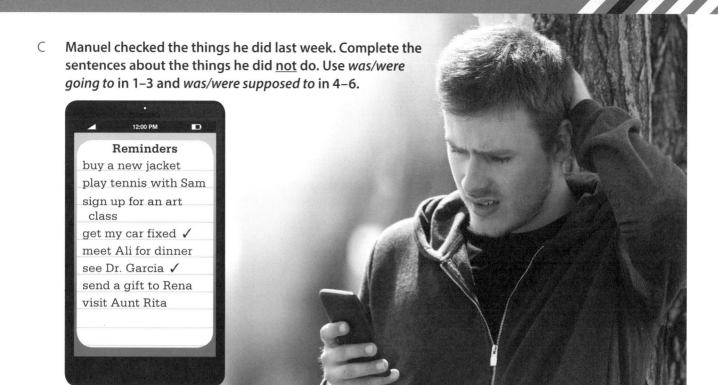

Reminders
buy a new jacket
play tennis with Sam
sign up for an art class
get my car fixed ✓
meet Ali for dinner
see Dr. Garcia ✓
send a gift to Rena
visit Aunt Rita

1   He was going to buy a new jacket _____, but he didn't.
2   _____, but he didn't.
3   _____, but he didn't.
4   _____, but he didn't.
5   _____, but he didn't.
6   _____, but he didn't.

3   GRAMMAR AND VOCABULARY

A   **Complete the sentences. Use the words in parentheses ( ) and the correct form of the phrasal verbs in the box.**

| cheer up | get together | go ahead | ~~hang out~~ |
| make up | mess up | split up | |

1   Luis and his friends _____ were going to hang out _____ (going to) at the mall last night, but the mall closed early.

2   I _____ (going to) with my friends for a movie, but I was held up.

3   The band _____ (going to) after their June concert, but they played together for one more year.

4   Charlie wasn't feeling well, but his parents _____ (going to) with the party. Then they changed their minds.

5   The party _____ (supposed to) Elisa, but it didn't. She was still sad.

6   Jessica _____ (going to) an excuse for missing the test. But in the end she told the truth.

7   Updating the operating system _____ (not supposed to) my phone, but it sure did. It won't even turn on now!

5.3 THERE MUST BE A MISTAKE!

1 FUNCTIONAL LANGUAGE: Reacting to bad news

A **Read the reactions to a problem. Circle the correct words. Then label each sentence** *reaction,* *escalation,* **or** *resolution.*

1 *There is /* (*Is there*) someone (*else*) */ more* I can speak to about this, please?   *escalation*

2 I *'m not / don't* get it.

3 I'm just glad *that / that's* settled.

4 *You can / Can you* check again, please?

5 *That's / This is* quite all right.

6 *Will / Would* you mind *take / taking* another look?

7 I don't *get / understand.*

8 There *can / must* be something you *can / must* do.

9 There *might / must* be *a / some* kind of mistake.

10 I *like / 'd like* to speak to *manager / the manager,* please.

2 REAL-WORLD STRATEGY: Accepting bad news

A **Put the words in order to complete the responses.**

1 **Salesperson** I can't lower the price of the car.

  You   that's not / to hear / but / what / can you / do / I hoped / what

                                                                      ?

2 **Server** I'm sorry, but there's no more chicken soup today.

  You   it / it / what / is / well / is

                                                                      .

3 **Manager** You can't leave work early today.

  You   life / well / that's

                                                                      .

4 **Dry cleaner** I'm sorry, but your jacket isn't ready yet.

  You   too / that's / bad

3 FUNCTIONAL LANGUAGE AND REAL-WORLD STRATEGY

A **Jason is in a store and is speaking to Alma at the cash register. Put the sentences in the correct order.**

Alma	The shirt is $50. It's $35 if you pay in cash.	_____
Alma	The sign says $35. Then in small letters it says "Cash."	_____
Jason	Here's my credit card for the shirt. It's $35, right?	1
Jason	There must be some kind of mistake. The sign says $35.	_____
Alma	The manager is busy. How about I give you this $15 tie for only $5?	_____
Jason	That's not right. Is there someone else I can speak to about this, please?	_____
Jason	Well, OK. I've never heard of a credit card difference in price, but I'm glad it's settled. Thanks.	_____

B **Read the situation. Then complete the conversation using the expressions from exercises 1A and 2A.**

Situation: Arturo lost his credit card yesterday. Today he checked online and noticed a lot of new charges on his credit card. He calls the credit card company to ask them to remove the charges and cancel his card.

Credit card worker	Max One credit card. How may I help you?
Arturo	Hi. I lost my credit card yesterday, and today there are some charges on my card that I didn't make. I'd like to have those charges removed and have my credit card canceled.
Credit card worker	Well, I can cancel your credit card, but I can't remove the charges, sir.
Arturo	_____
Credit card worker	I'm sorry sir, but there isn't. You will be responsible for those charges.
Arturo	_____
Credit card worker	Of course, sir. I'll transfer you right now.
Manager	Hello sir. How can I help you?
Arturo	Well, I'm trying to get some charges removed from my credit card account. I lost my card yesterday, and I guess someone else found it and used it.
Manager	I'm sorry to hear that. But since you didn't report your card as lost yesterday, I can't totally remove the charges. But I can reduce them by 50%.
Arturo	_____ .

5.4 THE PERFECT APOLOGY?

1 READING

A **Read the blog post about apologies. Does the writer think apologies matter a little or a lot? How do you know?**

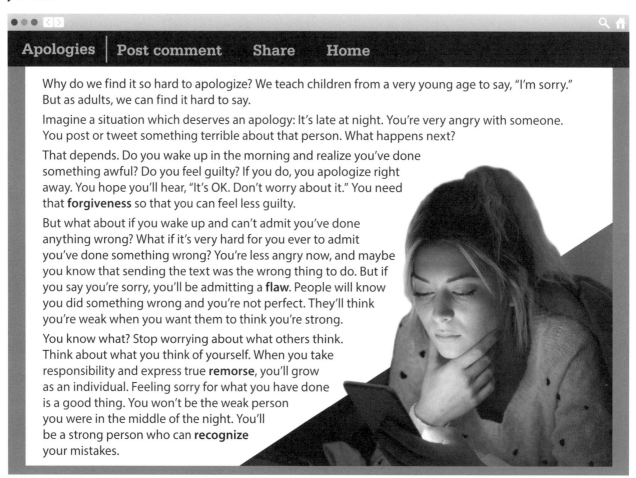

Apologies | **Post comment** | **Share** | **Home**

Why do we find it so hard to apologize? We teach children from a very young age to say, "I'm sorry." But as adults, we can find it hard to say.

Imagine a situation which deserves an apology: It's late at night. You're very angry with someone. You post or tweet something terrible about that person. What happens next?

That depends. Do you wake up in the morning and realize you've done something awful? Do you feel guilty? If you do, you apologize right away. You hope you'll hear, "It's OK. Don't worry about it." You need that **forgiveness** so that you can feel less guilty.

But what about if you wake up and can't admit you've done anything wrong? What if it's very hard for you ever to admit you've done something wrong? You're less angry now, and maybe you know that sending the text was the wrong thing to do. But if you say you're sorry, you'll be admitting a **flaw**. People will know you did something wrong and you're not perfect. They'll think you're weak when you want them to think you're strong.

You know what? Stop worrying about what others think. Think about what you think of yourself. When you take responsibility and express true **remorse**, you'll grow as an individual. Feeling sorry for what you have done is a good thing. You won't be the weak person you were in the middle of the night. You'll be a strong person who can **recognize** your mistakes.

B **UNDERSTANDING MEANING FROM CONTEXT** **Match the words from the reading (1–4) with their meaning (a–d). Then underline the words in the text that helped you guess the meaning.**

1 forgiveness _____ **a** the feeling that you are sorry for something bad you have done

2 flaw _____ **b** admit that something that is often unpleasant is true

3 remorse _____ **c** something about us that shows we are not perfect

4 recognize _____ **d** no longer being angry at someone who has done something bad to you

2 LISTENING

A 🔊 **5.01** **Listen to the conversation. Check (✓) the things the man and the woman mention.**

1 The man says what he did wrong. ☐

2 The woman gives advice about making apologies. ☐

3 The woman tells Marco words he should not use in an apology. ☐

4 The man says what happened after he apologized. ☐

3 WRITING

A Read the note of apology. Underline the parts where the writer uses the same language in two different sentences. Then replace the repeated words with words from the box.

> offer you this gift   ~~his behavior~~   his service

Apologies blog | Comment   Share   Messages   Notifications

Dear Ms. Vega,

Please accept my apologies for the way the server treated you last night. <u>The way the server treated you</u> *His behavior* was unacceptable. I have spoken to him, and I can promise you it will not happen again. I hope you will return to the restaurant so that I can give you a free meal. I would really like to give you a free meal because of what happened last night. I am truly sorry.

Sincerely,

Vincent Chu

B You are the owner of a clothing store. Last week, a sales clerk in your store was rude to a customer. Write an apology to the customer. Use the email in exercise 3A as an example.

_____

_____

_____

CHECK AND REVIEW

Read the statements. Can you do these things?

UNIT 5	Mark the boxes. ☑ I can do it. ? I am not sure. I can ...	If you are not sure, go back to these pages in the Student's Book.
VOCABULARY	☐ use specific terms to describe different types of stories.	page 44
	☐ use expressions to talk about making and breaking plans.	page 46
GRAMMAR	☐ order events in the past using the past perfect.	page 45
	☐ use *was/were going to* and *was/were supposed to* for plans in the past that changed or were cancelled.	page 47
FUNCTIONAL LANGUAGE	☐ react to problems and disappointing news.	page 48
	☐ accept bad news.	page 49
SKILLS	☐ write an apology.	page 51
	☐ avoid repetition in writing.	page 51

6.1 HELPING OUT

1 VOCABULARY: Describing communities

A **Complete the conversations with the words in the box.**

bring together	connect with	donate
get involved with	get to know	help out
join	pass on	take care of
~~take part in~~	volunteer	

1 A There's a community garden meeting next week. Would you want to go with me?

B Yes, I'd like to ____take part in____ that.

2 A Would you like to become a member of our organization?

B Yes, I'd really like to _____ .

3 A I was wondering if you'd like to give some money to our organization.

B Sure, I'd be happy to _____ .

4 A Who watches your children when you're at work?

B My parents _____ them.

5 A Do you have a lot of friends in your new neighborhood?

B Not really. I need to _____ more people.

6 A I don't get paid for the time I work at the hospital. I do it for free.

B It's very nice of you to _____ .

7 A My classmates and I have a lot in common.

B It's good that you have people you can _____ .

8 A Let me carry those boxes for you.

B It's very kind of you to _____ . Thank you.

9 A Let's have a street party so that all the neighbors can do things with each other.

B Yes, it will be good to _____ everyone in the neighborhood.

10 A These are the websites that will answer everyone's questions.

B OK, thanks. I'll _____ the information.

11 A Why did you start to volunteer at the after-school center?

B I wanted to _____ a group that helps children.

B **Complete the sentences so that they are true for you.**

1 I connect with people by ____talking about sports____ .

2 I've never donated to _____ , but I'd like to.

3 It would be fun to join _____ .

4 I want to get involved with _____ soon.

5 A good way to bring neighbors together is by _____ .

6 It's important to take care of _____ .

2   GRAMMAR: Present and past passives

A   **Underline the object of the sentence. Then rewrite the sentence using the present or past passive tense.**

1   Someone donated <u>millions of dollars</u>.
    Millions of dollars were donated.

2   People know the organization all over the world.
    _____

3   Someone started the shelter 50 years ago.
    _____

4   People give free clothes away every day.
    _____

5   Somebody serves the food three times a day.
    _____

6   People left their pets on the streets.
    _____

B   **Complete the sentences with passive verb forms. Use the verbs in parentheses ( ).**

1   I _____ _am given_ _____ (give) different things to do every week. That's why I like to volunteer.

2   We _____ (help) right away. It didn't take long for someone to see us.

3   The boys _____ (send) to a different room because they had arrived too late.

4   The students _____ (test) every Monday. They never like it.

5   A doctor _____ (call) when there is an emergency.

6   Our dog _____ (hit) by a car. We were so upset.

C   **Write yes/no and information questions. Use the passive. Then look online for the answers.**

1   where / the United Nations / found _Where was the United Nations founded?_
    It was founded in San Francisco in the United States.

2   when / the UN building in New York / complete
    _____

3   the UN building in New York / design / by a Brazilian architect
    _____

4   visitors to the UN building in New York / require / to get a
    security pass _____

5   tours of the UN / give / in English only
    _____

1 VOCABULARY: Describing good deeds

A **Circle the correct words.**

1 People should be *grateful* / *ungrateful* for the *kind* / *kindness* of others.

2 You can show your *appreciate* / *appreciation* by saying "thank you."

3 I'm sorry Tom was so *grateful* / *ungrateful* after all the *helpful* / *unhelpful* things you did for him.

4 The only *reward* / *rewarding* I want is your success. That will be very *reward* / *rewarding*.

5 Sometimes I get advice that is really *helpful* / *unhelpful*. People say things to me without thinking.

6 I *appreciate* / *appreciative* everything you have done for me.

7 We were very *appreciate* / *appreciative* of their *act* / *action* of kindness.

8 It was very *appreciative* / *thoughtful* of our neighbors to send food after the fire. I hope we showed our *grateful* / *gratitude*.

9 When you help someone with something, you are *lending a helping hand* / *showing your appreciation*.

10 It was a thoughtful gesture to *offer to help repair* / *think about repairing* the broken window.

B **Answer the questions. Use your own ideas.**

1 How do you show your appreciation for acts of kindness?

2 Who do you like to lend a helping hand to?

3 Why are thoughtful gestures important?

4 What kinds of things are you grateful for?

5 Do you think helping others is its own reward?

6 How do you react if someone is ungrateful for help you offer?

2 GRAMMAR: Passives with modals

A **Match 1–6 in column A with a–f in column B.**

A		B	
1	Animals here at the zoo should not ___c___	a	be remembered.
2	Your homework must _____	b	be taught to be polite.
3	Donations to the charity can _____	c	be given any kind of food.
4	New homes might _____	d	be found for the homeless.
5	Thank you so much for everything. Your kindness will _____	e	be finished by tonight.
6	Young children should _____	f	be sent at any time.

B **Complete the sentences using passives with modals. Use the words in parentheses ( ).**

1 Before you help people, they ___should be asked___ (should / ask) if they want help.

2 I promise that the report _____ (will / finish) before I leave.

3 This _____ (can't / do) by one person. You need help.

4 Tori _____ (might / give) a job at the animal shelter.

5 I think more money _____ (should / spend) on animals.

6 The boy's injury is serious. He _____ (must / take) to a hospital right away.

C **Answer the questions using passives with modals and the words in parentheses ( ). Then write another answer to the question using passives with modals and your own ideas.**

1 What can happen at home? (food / cook in a microwave oven)

   Food can be cooked in a microwave oven.

   Clothes can be washed in a washing machine.

2 What must happen at airports? (bags / check)

   _____

   _____

3 What should happen in parks? (children / watch)

   _____

   _____

4 What will happen in your next class? (we / give a homework assignment)

   _____

   _____

5 What might happen in stores? (customers / tell the wrong price)

   _____

   _____

THERE'S NO NEED ...

1 FUNCTIONAL LANGUAGE: Making offers

A Complete the conversations. Use the words in the box.
Write two more conversations using your own ideas.

anyway	appreciate	can	good
kind	let	like	manage

1 A Would you _____ to sit down?

 B I'm OK. Thanks _____.

2 A _____ I help you with those grocery bags?

 B Thanks, I really _____ it.

3 A _____ me get the door for you.

 B I can _____.

4 A Do you need a hand with that?

 B That's very _____ of you.

5 A I'm getting up. Do you want my seat?

 B Nope, it's all _____.

6 A _____

 B _____

7 A _____

 B _____

2 REAL-WORLD STRATEGY: Imposing on somebody

A What do the people request? Put the words in the correct order. Write a response either accepting or refusing the request. Then think of two more requests and responses.

1 I'm / but / sorry / is it / if / OK

 Ana _____ I use your phone for a moment?
 Mine is out of battery.

 _____.

2 I / don't / but / mind / rude / would you / to be / mean

 Joe _____ letting me go ahead of you in
 line? I only have a few items, and I'm in a rush.

 _____.

3 _____.

4 _____
 _____.

FUNCTIONAL LANGUAGE AND REAL-WORLD STRATEGY

A **Offer to help the person in the picture. Then write the person's response.**

1

A _____

B _____

2

A _____

B _____

3

A _____

B _____

4

A _____

B _____

B **Read the situations. Write a request and a response. Use *I'm really sorry to have to ask ...* or *I don't mean to be rude ...* to make the requests.**

1 Bernardo and Marta are co-workers. Their boss is waiting for their report by 5 p.m. but Bernardo gets a call that his son is sick. Bernardo has to leave. Marta doesn't have to leave.

A _____

B _____

2 Your car has broken down and won't be repaired for a few days. You need a car for a job interview tomorrow. Your neighbor has two cars.

A _____

B _____

6.4 PAINTING SAFER STREETS

1 LISTENING

A 🔊 **6.01** **LISTEN FOR GIST** **Listen to the conversation about guerilla gardening. Check (✓) the topics that Angela mentions.**

What guerilla gardening is ☐

Why she started guerilla gardening ☐

The places she has done guerilla gardening ☐

Other countries where guerilla gardening happens ☐

Some of the problems with guerilla gardening ☐

B 🔊 **6.01** **LISTEN FOR DETAIL** **Listen again. Write *T* (true) or *F* (false).**

1 Greg and Angela both do guerrilla gardening. _F_

2 People do guerrilla gardening to improve public spaces. ___

3 City governments help with guerrilla gardening projects. ___

4 People can send donations if they want to support guerrilla gardening. ___

5 Guerrilla gardening groups exist only in North America. ___

6 Businesses are helping guerilla gardening groups. ___

2 READING

A **Read about guerrilla gardening in Los Angeles, California. Circle the correct answers.**

> Guerrilla gardening started back in the 1970s and has grown into an international movement. In some places, people do it to make public spaces more beautiful; in other places, they do it to grow food. In South Central Los Angeles, it was very difficult in the past to find healthy food. That's why a movement was started to grow vegetable gardens on city property. An organization, L.A. Green Grounds, was formed and started planting fruit trees and vegetables. The gardeners were all volunteers and came from all over the city and many different professions. Green Grounds has helped to change a community. There is plenty more space that could be improved. The city of Los Angeles owns nearly 26 square miles of empty land. That's enough land to plant 725 million tomato plants!

1 Guerrilla gardening started *a few /(many)*years ago

2 In the past, people had to drive far to buy *fast food / healthy food.*

3 L.A. Green Grounds was started in order to *make the community beautiful / grow food.*

4 Volunteers for L.A. Green Grounds *all live / do not all live* in South Central Los Angeles.

5 The city of Los Angeles *owns / does not own* a lot of empty land.

3 WRITING

A Read the report. Find the quotations and circle the phrases that are used to introduce them. Then underline the verbs that are used in the phrases.

> The city has a lot of empty space that could be used for guerrilla gardening. A recent report by Our Community Together has made a list of the possible places. One of the leaders of the group claimed that "many parts of the city are ugly because nobody takes care of them. Using those spaces to grow plants will make the city more beautiful."
>
> When asked for comment, one resident said, "I think this is an excellent idea. We could start with the Greenwood section of town. Right now it is full of trash. It should be cleaned up."
>
> However, not everybody agrees. One person in city government pointed out that "the city has a lot of needs. The empty space could be used for day-care centers and libraries."
>
> It is true that cities have many needs, but we must accept that having beautiful spaces is one of those needs.

B Think of an empty space in your town that guerrilla gardening could improve. Write a report about the space. Write about where it is, how big it is, what the space looks like right now, and how it could be changed. Include at least one quotation. You can make up the quotation.

CHECK AND REVIEW

Read the statements. Can you do these things?

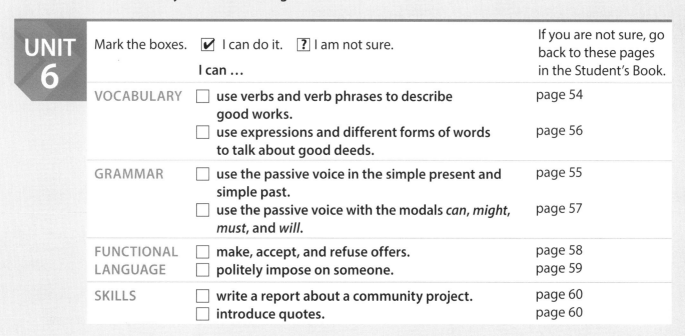

UNIT 6	Mark the boxes. ✔ I can do it. ? I am not sure. I can …	If you are not sure, go back to these pages in the Student's Book.
VOCABULARY	☐ use verbs and verb phrases to describe good works.	page 54
	☐ use expressions and different forms of words to talk about good deeds.	page 56
GRAMMAR	☐ use the passive voice in the simple present and simple past.	page 55
	☐ use the passive voice with the modals *can*, *might*, *must*, and *will*.	page 57
FUNCTIONAL LANGUAGE	☐ make, accept, and refuse offers.	page 58
	☐ politely impose on someone.	page 59
SKILLS	☐ write a report about a community project.	page 60
	☐ introduce quotes.	page 60

1   VOCABULARY: Describing communication

A   **Use the words in the box to describe the quotes.
Sometimes there is more than one correct answer.**

catch up with	~~congratulate~~	criticize for
explain	gossip	keep in touch with
persuade to	reply	respond to

1 We were so excited to hear about the new baby. We're so happy for you!

congratulate

2 Well, I got a new job, and the baby is now walking! What's new with you?

3 Well, the reason that I was late was that my car broke down.

4 I just got your message. Yes, I will buy milk and bread.

5 Here are all the reasons we should get a dog.

6 Mike didn't do a great job on this report. He made several mistakes.

7 Hey. It's been a while since we talked, so I figured I'd call and say "hi."

8 Did you hear the news? Diana and Bernardo have broken up.

B   **Circle the correct words to complete the sentences.**

1   No one *informed / contacted* me that the date of the party had changed.

2   Raquel was angry until Eduardo *gossiped / explained* that the reason he missed the party was that he was sick.

3   Julio didn't know about the hurricane until he saw it *reported / informed* on TV.

4   While we were catching up, Ben also *mentioned / recalled* that he got a new dog.

2   GRAMMAR: Reported speech

A   **Read the conversation. Then circle the correct words. Sometimes both words are correct.**

Emma	I like your hat.	**1**	Emma *said /* (told) Amin that she *likes /* (liked) his hat.
Amin	I have had it for a long time.	**2**	Amin *said / told* that he *has / had had* it for a long time.
Emma	Well, it's very nice.	**3**	Emma *said / told* that it *is / was* very nice.
Amin	I've been ill.	**4**	Amin *said / told* Emma that he *is / had been* ill.
Emma	I'm sorry to hear that.	**5**	Emma *said / told* that she *was / has been* sorry to hear that.
Amin	I still don't feel well.	**6**	Amin *said / told* that he still *doesn't feel / didn't feel* well.

B **Rewrite the sentences in reported speech.**

1 "I haven't gotten any messages in a week."

   She said that she hadn't gotten any messages in a week.

2 "Sorry I'm late. I didn't know where to go."

   He told us _____ .

3 "I haven't really kept in touch with Mike."

   She said that _____ .

4 "I'm trying to persuade my husband to get a dog."

   She told us that _____ .

5 "My boss criticized me for being late a couple times last week."

   He explained that _____ .

6 "I don't recall having sent that email."

   He claimed that _____ .

3 GRAMMAR AND VOCABULARY

A **Report what the people said. Replace *said* or *told* with one of the verbs in the box.**

commented	~~explained~~	informed	persuaded	recalled	replied	reported

1 "Jake needs to fill in two different forms," Risa said.

   Risa explained that Jake needed to fill in two different forms.

2 "No, I haven't been able to contact Jane," Yumi said.

   _____

3 "The post is very funny," Victor said.

   _____

4 "There was an accident at your home in the morning," the police officer told Mr. Santiago.

   _____

5 "Take plenty of warm clothes on your trip," Sara told John. (He did what she said.)

   _____

6 Mike said, "In 1998, I saw the Statue of Liberty."

   _____

7 "You paid too much in taxes last year," the accountant said.

   _____

7.2 TO TEXT OR NOT TO TEXT

1 VOCABULARY: Talking about online communication

A **Complete the definitions with the words in the box.**

| clickbait | geo-tag | hashtag | ~~lurker~~ | meme | newsfeed |
| podcaster | profile | status update | tag | timeline | trending topic |

1 A _____lurker_____ reads other people's comments and posts, but doesn't make their own comments or posts.

2 _____ is an article that is designed to get attention but that may not be true.

3 A _____ shows information about important things happening around the world.

4 You can find someone's photos and posts on their _____ .

5 A _____ is a piece of information (usually funny) that spreads very quickly on the Internet.

6 A _____ is something that a lot of people are currently posting about.

7 When you _____ a photo online, people know where the picture was taken.

8 When you post a _____ , you put new information online about yourself.

9 Your _____ has a description of you and your interests on a website.

10 When you _____ something online, you add information to it.

11 A _____ helps to connect an online post with other posts on the same topic.

12 If you are a _____ you host an online talk show.

2 GRAMMAR: Reporting questions

A **Put the words in the reported questions in the correct order.**

1 social media / asked / use / I / she / how often

   ~~She asked how often I use social media.~~

2 social media / asked / my parents / he / what / visited / sites / they

   _____ .

3 were / she / my favorite / what / blogs / asked

   _____ .

4 me / they / an iPad / used / if / asked / I / in high school / had

   _____ .

5 him / he / I / had / asked / met / if / anyone online

   _____
   _____ .

6 if / comment / asked / to / on / me / liked / videos / they / I

   _____
   _____ .

52

B   **Write the direct questions from exercise 2A.**

1   *How often do you use social media?*

2   _____

3   _____

4   _____

5   _____

6   _____

3 **GRAMMAR AND VOCABULARY**

A   **An interviewer asked Maria questions. Complete her answers with words from exercise 1A.**

1   Maria replied, "No, I never _____tag_____ myself in my photos."

2   "I use _____ because more people see my ideas that way."

3   "I _____ my photos so people can see where I've been."

4   "I update my professional _____ every six months."

5   "No, I don't get all of my news from _____."

6   "My favorite _____ is Francine Veronica. I love her show."

7   "I often read about _____, since everyone is talking about them."

8   "I only share _____ that I think are funny and harmless."

B   **Report the questions the interviewer asked.**

1   *The interviewer asked Maria if she ever tagged herself in her photos.*

2   _____

3   _____

4   _____

5   _____

6   _____

7   _____

8   _____

AND I'M LIKE ...

1 FUNCTIONAL LANGUAGE: Recounting stories

A Complete the conversations. Use the phrases in the box.

> Apparently   ~~I heard that~~   What happened was that
> Who told you that   Wow, that's terrible

Gloria So how was Tom's 30th birthday party? ¹ _I heard that_ Tom's brother, Steve, didn't go. ² _____, he had the flu. He was too sick to get out of bed.

Hope ³ _____? That's all wrong. ⁴ _____ we had to change where the party was going to be. And anyway, nobody thought to call Steve and tell him. That's why he missed the party.

Gloria ⁵ _____!

> in the end   it turns out that   someone told me that   was like   what happened was that

Ray Did you hear what happened to Ahsan last week?

Ivan ⁶ _____ he got fired for yelling at his boss.

Ray No, no, no. You see ⁷ _____ his boss told him he had to work over the weekend. And Ahsan ⁸ _____, "I can't. It's my daughter's birthday." Well, his boss told him that he had to work anyway, and Ahsan got mad and quit.

Ivan Really? Wow. That's too bad for Ahsan.

Ray Maybe not. You see, ⁹ _____ he was already thinking about looking for a new job. So, ¹⁰ _____ it might be for the best.

> apparently   it turns out that   the funny thing is
> you'll never believe this   what happened was

Natasha Hey Vince. Did you hear about Sara?

Vince No. What?

Natasha ¹¹ _____, but she got married last weekend!

Vince Get out of here! I didn't even know she was dating anyone.

Natasha ¹² _____ she wasn't. ¹³ _____ she went to her high school reunion last month, and her old boyfriend was there. ¹⁴ _____ she still had feelings for him after all these years, and ¹⁵ _____ he felt the same way about her. So anyway, now they're married.

Vince Well good for them. I hope it works out.

2 REAL-WORLD STRATEGY: Getting back on track

A Complete the conversation with the words in the box.

I lost my train of thought	so, as I was saying	what was I saying	where was I? Oh yeah,

Irina   Last night I couldn't get my daughter to put her tablet down.

Megan   How is Olive? I heard that she won the swimming competition last week.

Irina   Yeah. It was great. We were proud of her. Sorry, ¹_____? So she wouldn't put the tablet away, and I was getting really annoyed. I wanted her to help clean up, and she'd been chatting with her friend Julia for hours.

Megan   I know exactly how you feel. Josh never helps clean up either.

Irina   It's super frustrating, right? ²_____, she'd been chatting with her friend for hours and still wouldn't put the tablet away. So eventually, I took it and told her she couldn't have it back for a week.

Megan   Ha! I'll bet that caused a fight.

Irina   You better believe it. So she was yelling and screaming, and uh …

Megan   Right, so she was yelling and screaming …

Irina   Right. Sorry, ³_____. So anyway my husband comes in, like right in the middle of this, and gives her the tablet back! I couldn't believe it. I was so angry.

Megan   I got angry with Mario last night. He was late for dinner, and I missed my meeting.

Irina   That's too bad. So, ⁴_____ David and I got into a big argument and now we're not talking to each other.

3 FUNCTIONAL LANGUAGE AND REAL-WORLD STRATEGY

A Imagine you know the woman in the picture. Make up a story about what happened to her. Write a conversation telling a friend about it. Your friend interrupts at least one time. Begin like this:

You   *You'll never believe what happened to* _____

Friend _____

You   _____

Friend _____

You   _____

Friend _____

You   _____

Friend _____

1   READING

A   **READ FOR MAIN IDEA**   Read the post. Underline the sentences that express the writer's main idea.

| Emojis \| | Blog | Add comment | Share |

Are you someone like me who resists using emojis? Can you not understand why people prefer silly images over meaningful words? Well, I have news for you: You and I are the problem, not emojis. The world has moved on, and you and I must, too. Here's why:

Emojis are global. When people speak different languages, they find it hard to communicate. But emojis mean the same thing to everyone. It doesn't matter if they speak Chinese, English, or Spanish.

Emojis are a big part of social media. Emojis are all over social media. In some platforms, they are over 40% of text. In a few years, they will likely be over 50%. Future communication is certain to have more emojis and fewer words. People find emojis a simpler and faster way to communicate.

Emojis are part of our everyday lives. Now you can order pizza 🍕 with emojis in a Tweet. What will be next – ✈️ plane tickets? Why not?

Language changes slowly, but it is always happening. Emojis are part of today's change. They are here to stay, until the next change. 😬

B   **READ FOR OPINIONS**   Read the post again. Circle the correct words to complete the statements.

1   The writer believes that people who resist using emojis *have good reasons / are part of the problem*.

2   The writer says that emojis are *helpful / unhelpful* when people speak different languages.

3   The writer believes that emojis *may be / will definitely be* more common in the future.

2   LISTENING

A   🔊 **7.01**   Listen to a discussion about using emojis in the classroom. Read the opinions. Write *G* for Gina's opinion, *K* for Ken's opinion, *B* for both, or *X* if something is not mentioned.

1   Emojis improve communication.   *G*

2   Emojis help make creative work easier and more fun.   _____

3   Students like what is familiar. That's why they prefer to use emojis to learn language.   _____

4   Emojis can help with students who have clear communication difficulties.   _____

5   Emojis can't help students understand difficult material like Shakespeare.   _____

6   Just because students are interested doesn't mean they learn something well.   _____

7   There are more benefits from using emojis for younger students than older ones.   _____

8   There are many different kinds of activities students can do with emojis.   _____

3 WRITING

A Write an informal email that does the following: tells the person you are going to miss a meeting, apologizes, and suggests a new time for the meeting.

_____

_____

_____

_____

_____

_____

B Now write a formal email that contains the same information from exercise 3A.

_____

_____

_____

_____

_____

_____

_____

CHECK AND REVIEW

Read the statements. Can you do these things?

UNIT 7	Mark the boxes. ☑ I can do it. ? I am not sure. I can ...	If you are not sure, go back to these pages in the Student's Book.
VOCABULARY	☐ use verbs and verb phrases to describe communication.	page 66
	☐ use terms for different types of online communication.	page 68
GRAMMAR	☐ report statements that were made in different tenses.	page 67
	☐ report questions that were asked in different tenses.	page 69
FUNCTIONAL LANGUAGE	☐ recount conversations, news, and stories.	page 70
	☐ get back on track after an interruption.	page 71
SKILLS	☐ write a formal and an informal email.	page 73

8.1 THE PERFECT JOB?

1 VOCABULARY: Describing jobs

A **Cross out the word that does <u>not</u> naturally follow the adjective.**

1 challenging:	work	day	job	~~vacation~~
2 high-paying:	position	employee	job	company
3 freelance:	company	job	position	worker
4 permanent:	career	employee	position	job
5 stressful:	boss	day	job	time
6 temporary:	job	friend	employee	place to live
7 tiring:	day	work	sleep	vacation
8 tough:	boss	job	fun	life

B **Complete the sentences. Use the words in the box.**

> desk job dream job full-time job ~~government job~~
> main job part-time jobs second job

1 Teri is an accountant for the city of New York. She has a _____*government job*_____ .

2 Magda wants to work 40 hours a week, but she can't find a _____ . Instead, she's working two _____ : one in a store for 15 hours a week and one in a restaurant for 20 hours a week.

3 Hector enjoys working with his hands and working outdoors. That's why he's so unhappy with his

_____ .

4 Suki's a high school teacher. That's her _____ . But she needs more money, so she has a _____ . She works in a restaurant on weekends and during summer vacation.

5 I love traveling and I love boats. So my _____ would be to work on a cruise ship and see the world.

2 GRAMMAR: Unreal present conditionals

A **Match 1–6 in column A with a–f in column B.**

A

1 If I didn't need the money, ____*e*____
2 I'd invest in a new product if _____
3 If I had a lot of free time, _____
4 I'd get together with friends more if _____
5 If I ran my own business, _____
6 I might take a salary cut if _____

B

a I might get a second job.
b I'd be a great boss.
c I wanted to work less.
d I had money in the bank.
e I wouldn't work two jobs.
f I weren't working all the time.

Put the words in order to form unreal conditional sentences.

1 big house / if / I would / I lived / have / lots of space / in a

   If I lived in a big house, I would have lots of space. OR I would have lots of space if I lived in a big house.

2 if / to the beach / didn't rain / more often / so much / it / we / would go

   _____

3 my neighborhood / always / so noisy / there / weren't / a lot of traffic / wouldn't be / if

   _____

4 far away / miss them / my family / lived / I / would / if

   _____

5 a dog / allergies / I would / didn't / if / get / I / have

   _____

3 GRAMMAR AND VOCABULARY

A **Write an unreal conditional sentence to show the opposite of each situation. Then write two more conditional sentences using the words from exercises 1A and 1B.**

1 I don't live in a big house. I don't have a lot of space.

   If I lived in a big house, I would have a lot of space. OR I would have a lot of space if I lived in a big house.

2 My job is only part-time. I don't earn a lot of money.

   _____

3 My job is very challenging. I'm always tired when I get home.

   _____

4 My job is far away. It's not my dream job.

   _____

5 I don't work freelance. I am not my own boss.

   _____

6 I have a desk job. My job is very boring.

   _____

7 _____

8 _____

8.2 FINDING A BALANCE

1 VOCABULARY: Talking about work/life balance

A **Circle the correct answers.**

1 My <u>family life</u> is the *place I live / (time I spend)* with my family.
2 When you have <u>me time</u>, you *do things with others / relax on your own*.
3 When you have <u>downtime</u>, you *don't do very much / have a little time*.
4 If you have a <u>9 to 5</u> job, you spend most of the *day / night* in an office.
5 When you take <u>time off</u>, you are *doing / not doing* your usual work or studies.
6 At a <u>seminar</u>, a *large / small* group of people have a discussion with a teacher or expert.
7 Someone who is <u>always connected</u> can do things on *the Internet / a phone* all the time.
8 When you have an <u>assignment</u>, someone has given you work you *like to / have to* do.
9 If you have a <u>busy schedule</u>, you *have / don't have* a lot of free time.
10 When you work the *day / night* <u>shift</u>, you might work from 4 p.m. to midnight.
11 During a <u>lecture</u>, the professor speaks for *less / more* than ten minutes.
12 During <u>office hours</u>, professors often *talk to / test* their students.
13 When you have a busy <u>social life</u>, you spend a lot of time with your *co-workers / friends*.
14 When you have a <u>commitment</u>, you have something you *must / want to* do.

2 GRAMMAR: *I wish*

A **Read the sentences. Do they express present, past, or future wishes?**

1 I wish I had more time to study.   _present_
2 I wish I hadn't bought these shoes.   _____
3 I wish you hadn't moved away.   _____
4 I wish I didn't have to work next week.   _____
5 I wish I could go to the party tonight.   _____
6 I wish you had told me the truth.   _____
7 I wish I weren't living downtown.   _____
8 I wish you were here.   _____

B **Write the correct form of the verb in parentheses ( ).**

1 I wish I _____could go_____ (can go) with you, but I have to stay home with the kids.

2 I wish I _____ (not buy) these shoes online. I don't like them, and I can't return them.

3 I wish I _____ (not take) the final exam next week. I need more time to study.

4 I wish I _____ (have) time to go to the party. I really don't want to miss it.

5 I wish I _____ (not have to) move. I know this apartment is small, but I really love it.

6 I wish I _____ (live) closer to my job. Then I could walk to work.

7 I wish I _____ (go) somewhere else for my vacation. It rained every day at the beach.

8 I wish I _____ (not say) that. It was rude. I'm sorry.

3 GRAMMAR AND VOCABULARY

A **Write sentences that are true for you. Use *wish* and the phrases in the box.**

(not) be always connected	have a (better) family life	have (more) time off
have a (more exciting) social life	~~have (more) downtime~~	(not) have a lot of commitments
(not) have a 9 to 5 job	take it easy (more)	(not) have a busy schedule
(not) work the night shift		

1 I wish I had more downtime at work.

2 _____

3 _____

4 _____

5 _____

6 _____

7 _____

8 _____

9 _____

10 _____

61

I WOULDN'T DO THAT!

1 FUNCTIONAL LANGUAGE: Discuss options

A **Match 1–8 in column A with a–h in column B.**

A			B	
1	I would if	_f_	a	I were you.
2	Have you		b	you can do it next week?.
3	It can't		c	you could offer to talk about the problem.
4	You might		d	to lose.
5	Maybe		e	tried talking to someone about the problem?
6	I'd try that if		f	I were in your shoes.
7	You have nothing		g	want to suggest another solution.
8	Is there anyway		h	hurt, right?

2 REAL-WORLD STRATEGY: Negative advice

A **Correct the mistakes in the responses.**

1 **A** I'm going to leave my phone in the car.

   B You don't want do that.

   You don't want to do that.

2 **A** I'm going to stay home on the day of the exam.

   B I couldn't do that if I were you!

3 **A** I'm going to complain to the boss about the job.

   B You might to not want to do that.

4 **A** I'm going to lie to Sam about where I was last night.

   B I'll avoid that if I were you.

5 **A** I'm going to tell my son that I don't like his new girlfriend.

   B I wouldn't do that if I was you.

6 **A** I'm going to change my email password to 12345.

   B I'd avoid that if I'd were you.

3 FUNCTIONAL LANGUAGE AND REAL-WORLD STRATEGY

A **Read the statements. Write advice.**

1 **A** I have real sleeping problems. Some nights I don't fall asleep for two hours.

   B *Have you tried drinking warm milk? I've heard that helps.*

2 **A** My pants don't fit well. I'm not going to eat any bread, meat, or fruit until they fit again.

   B *I wouldn't do that if I were you! A healthy diet includes all types of foods.*

3 **A** I can't believe I'm still living at home. I wish I could afford to get my own place.

   B _____

4 **A** I can't seem to find a permanent job. For the past two years I've only gotten temporary ones.

   B _____

5 **A** I have a 9 to 5 job that I really hate. I'm so bored that I want to quit.

   B _____

6 **A** I've been working the night shift for two years. I've asked to work the day shift a few times, but I never get it.

   B _____

7 **A** I'm going to take a trip around the world. I don't have much money, but I've heard it's not too hard to find work in other countries.

   B _____

8 **A** I moved here six months ago and still don't know anyone. I'm lonely.

   B _____

9 **A** I owe a friend some money, but I can't pay him back.

   B _____

10 **A** A good friend of mine is depressed. I don't know what to do.

   B _____

DIGITAL DETOX

1 LISTENING

A 🔊 **8.01** Listen to the conversation. What made Selena's digital detox successful?

B 🔊 **8.01** **LISTEN FOR ATTITUDE** Listen again. Write *T* (true) or *F* (false) for each statement.

1 Selena understands why Josh thinks she didn't enjoy her vacation. _____

2 Josh is surprised that Selena's digital detox worked. _____

3 Selena doesn't understand why Josh doubts the digital detox app. _____

4 At the end of the conversation, Josh changes his opinion of the digital detox app. _____

2 READING

A **Read the text. Check (✓) the benefits the writer mentions.**

The benefits of turning off your phone

A recent study has shown that we touch our phones 80 times a day on average. That is a shocking number, and it can't be good for us. Here are three ways turning off our phones can help us:

1. We are on our phones so much that we are filling our heads with unimportant information. We're not using our eyes to notice who and what is around us. Studies have shown that we get ideas from noticing things. If our brains are filled with unimportant things and not with new things we see around us, we have fewer new ideas.

2. People feel less stress when they stop using their phones all the time. They also sleep better. You certainly don't need your phone in your bedroom. Buy an old-fashioned alarm clock. It will do as good a job waking you up in the morning.

3. Having a conversation with someone is much better than 50 texts or 10 emails. This is especially true at work where co-workers get more things done and get them done faster when they talk face to face. People understand each other better and trust each other more.

1 Better education ☐
2 Better health ☐
3 Better ideas ☐
4 Better jobs ☐
5 Better relationships ☐

A **Read the comments that listeners left on the podcast web page. Look at the underlined phrases. Then choose the correct answer.**

Comments

1 This week's podcast was really interesting. To be honest, I hadn't thought a lot about how often I use my phone. <u>As you said</u>, it's strange that my friends and I get together and then spend so much of the time looking at our phones. I have a question about where to go for digital detox. <u>You point out that</u> it is a good idea to go to a place where everybody is trying to do a digital detox. Does it matter if the people are friends or strangers? I mean, if a friend of mine wants to do a digital detox, could we go together or would that be a bad idea? I look forward to hearing your reply!

2 I really enjoyed this week's podcast. <u>There was one thing in particular that interested me.</u> I never knew there were places that focus on technology-free experiences. I was wondering if you could give me the names of two or three places like that.

These people use the underlined phrases to:

A give an opinion about what he or she heard in the podcast.

B refer to a statement or opinion he or she heard in the podcast.

B **Write a comment about the conversation you heard in exercise 1A. Use phrases that reference the speakers' statements or opinions.**

CHECK AND REVIEW

Read the statements. Can you do these things?

UNIT 8	Mark the boxes. ☑ I can do it. ? I am not sure. I can …	If you are not sure, go back to these pages in the Student's Book.
VOCABULARY	☐ use adjectives to describe jobs and work situations.	page 76
	☐ discuss factors related to a healthy work/life balance.	page 78
GRAMMAR	☐ use present unreal conditionals.	page 77
	☐ express dissatisfaction with *I wish*.	page 79
FUNCTIONAL LANGUAGE	☐ discuss options.	page 80
	☐ offer a warning.	page 81
SKILLS	☐ write a comment about a podcast.	page 83
	☐ make reference to points other people make.	page 83

1 VOCABULARY: Talking about places

A **Write the place under each picture. The first letter of each word is given to you.**

1 toll
   plaza

2 r
   a

3 b

4 c

5 p

6 c

7 c
   s

8 r
   s

9 l

B **Cross out the word that does not belong.**

1 Government buildings:	city hall	construction site	courthouse	consulate
2 City buildings:	arts center	city hall	consulate	rest stop
3 Outdoor areas:	boardwalk	laboratory	playground	public space

2 GRAMMAR: Prohibition, permission, obligation (present)

A **Circle the correct answer.**

1 You *aren't allowed to* / *aren't required to* wear shorts in the swimming pool.

2 You *are allowed to* / *are required to* have a passport for international travel.

3 You *are allowed to* / *are supposed to* arrive at the airport at least an hour before departure.

4 You *are supposed to* / *may not* use your phone during the exam. If you do, you will fail.

5 You *are allowed to* / *shouldn't* eat and drink during the break, but not during class.

6 You *may* / *must* leave the meeting early if you want to.

B **Complete the sentences. Use the verbs in parentheses ( ) and (*not*) *be allowed to*, (*not*) *be supposed to*, (*not*) *be required to*, or *may* (*not*).**

1 There's a stop sign. You _____are required to stop_____ (stop).

2 You _____ (charge) your phone here. The sign says it's OK.

3 On the day of the exam, you _____ (leave) your phone at home. If you don't, the teacher will take it away.

4 You _____ (turn) right when the sign says "no right turn."

5 All students _____ (take) the final exam. They can't pass the course without it.

6 I _____ (be) here until 9 o'clock. I hope it's OK that I'm a little early.

3 GRAMMAR AND VOCABULARY

A **Write rules for each place. Use (*not*) *be allowed to*, (*not*) *be supposed to*, (*not*) *be required to* or *may* (*not*).**

1 airport terminal (prohibition)
   You are not allowed to go through security without a ticket.

2 boardwalk (permission)
   _____

3 city hall (obligation)
   _____

4 construction site (obligation)
   _____

5 courthouse (permission)
   _____

6 consulate (prohibition)
   _____

7 public space (permission)
   _____

8 residential area (prohibition)
   _____

1   VOCABULARY: Talking about rules

A   **Write *N* if the underlined part of the sentence is a noun. Write *V* if it is a verb.**

1   Your car needs <u>to be registered</u>.   _V_
2   Where's the <u>registration</u>?   _N_
3   You <u>are not permitted</u> to park here. _____
4   There's a <u>ban</u> on noise after 11 p.m. _____
5   He lost <u>control</u> of the car and hit a tree. _____
6   The rule <u>limits</u> the number of cars. _____
7   There's a <u>prohibition</u> on smoking here. _____
8   Cars <u>are banned</u> from some parts of the downtown area. _____

9   You have my <u>permission</u> to go. _____
10   We <u>are required</u> to leave by 8. _____
11   I know my <u>limits</u>. _____
12   He <u>is prohibited</u> from entering. _____
13   It's your <u>obligation</u> to help. _____
14   Driving school isn't a <u>requirement</u>. _____
15   We <u>are obliged</u> to have a license. _____
16   Who <u>controls</u> the parking lot? _____

B   **Complete the sentences with words from exercise 1A.**

1   Your life changes when you become a parent, because parents have many ____obligations____ .
2   There's a temporary _____ on soccer fans at the stadium. They are not allowed to attend any games.
3   There's a _____ on the number of students we can accept. This year we can't take more than 20.
4   Parents should _____ their children's behavior.
5   It is not a _____ to take English 1 before English 2, but it is a good idea.
6   Nobody is _____ to leave the building until the police say it is OK to do so.

C   **Complete the sentences with your ideas.**

1   If I were the leader of my country, it would be a requirement for people to _____vote_____ .
2   There should be a ban on _____ .
3   If I were the teacher, I would limit _____ .
4   I don't think children should be permitted to _____ .
5   I don't think governments should control _____ .
6   The prohibition against _____ should be removed.

2 GRAMMAR: Prohibition, permission, obligation (past)

A Write the missing words.

1 I _____could_____ not play after school when I was young.

2 Victor was _____ to work last weekend, so he couldn't go to the game.

3 Were you allowed _____ eat candy when you were a child?

4 I _____ supposed to wear a suit at my last job, but sometimes I didn't.

5 The kids were _____ to play in the park until their parents came to get them. They always had fun.

6 Did you _____ to move, or did you move because you wanted to?

B Write about the bike race Mario was in last month. Use *(not) allowed to, could (not), had to, supposed to,* and *required to.*

Rules of the Race

1 Mario _____was allowed to_____ ride with a team.

2 Mario _____ stop another cyclist.

3 He _____ wear a helmet.

4 He _____ stop for water.

5 _____ have a second bike.

6 _____ cross the yellow line.

C Rewrite the sentences. Use the words in parentheses ( ). Then check (✓) any sentences that used to be true in your country.

1 It was a requirement for a child to start school at the age of 4. (require) ☐

   A child was required to start school at the age of 4.

2 Students had to stand when the teacher entered the room. (require) ☐

   _____

3 It was necessary for students to wait until the teacher called on them before they spoke. (supposed to) ☐

   _____

4 Children could play in the streets until nighttime. (allow) ☐

   _____

5 A child couldn't talk when the family was having a meal. (allow) ☐

   _____

9.3 TO TIP OR NOT TO TIP?

1 FUNCTIONAL LANGUAGE: Making generalizations

A **Correct the mistakes in the sentences.**

1 I ~~general~~ *generally* don't eat a big breakfast.

2 I tend have just a cup of coffee.

3 On whole, mealtime isn't very important to me.

4 Generally speak, I don't eat dinner with my family.

5 In average, I eat with my family once or twice a week.

B **Complete the conversation. Sometimes there may be more than one answer.**

A Let me be the first one to say welcome to the company.

B Thank you. I'm really happy to be here.

A I know it's your first day, so do you have any questions?

B Uh, yeah a couple. Is there a dress code?

A ¹_____ , no. You can dress pretty casually – unless we have a big meeting scheduled or something like that.

B That's good to know. What about start times? Do most people ²_____ have a 9 to 5 schedule, or do some people start later or earlier?

A ³_____ , it's 9 to 5. But if there's a reason you need to work a different schedule, we can talk about it.

B No, 9 to 5 works fine for me. I was just curious. What about lunch? How much time do people take?

A ⁴_____ , about 30 minutes. Some people take a full hour and work a little later, though.

2 REAL-WORLD STRATEGY: Contrasting information

A **Read what speaker A says. Put the words in speaker B's response in the correct order. Which are true for you?**

1 **A** We tip 20% to a hairdresser.

   B that / nearly / don't / much / tip / as / we / as

   We don't tip nearly as much as that.

2 **A** Strangers shake hands when they meet.

   B country / we / do / that / don't / in / it / way / my

   _____

3 **A** Friends kiss each other twice when they meet.

   B really? / that / do / we / where / from / don't / come / I

   _____

4 **A** Workers get five weeks of vacation every year.

   B back / differently / things / home / we / do

   _____

FUNCTIONAL LANGUAGE AND REAL-WORLD STRATEGY

A **Read Mathilde's comments about the French way of life. Respond with generalizations about your country.**

1 **Mathilde:** On average, French people work 35 hours a week.

On average, in Japan we work more than 40 hours a week.

2 **Mathilde:** On the whole, children in my region go to school four and a half days a week.

You: _____

3 **Mathilde:** Generally speaking, French people go on vacation in August.

You: _____

4 **Mathilde:** French people generally don't eat a sandwich for lunch.

You: _____

5 **Mathilde:** Young people tend to live with their parents until they're in their twenties.

You: _____

6 **Mathilde:** In general, French restaurants are open from noon to 2 p.m. and from 7 p.m. to 9 p.m.

You: _____

B **Check (✓) the generalizations about mealtime that are the same in your country. Write contrasting information for the sentences you do not check.**

1 We eat our main meal at noon. ☐

We do things differently back home. We eat our main meal at 6 in the evening.

2 In general, people eat cheese at the end of meals. ☐

3 We never have a meal without bread. ☐

4 Generally speaking, the whole family eats together on Sundays. ☐

5 Meals can last six hours. ☐

THE STORY OF THE RAMP

1 READING

A **Read the article. Who are Oscar and Mimi?**

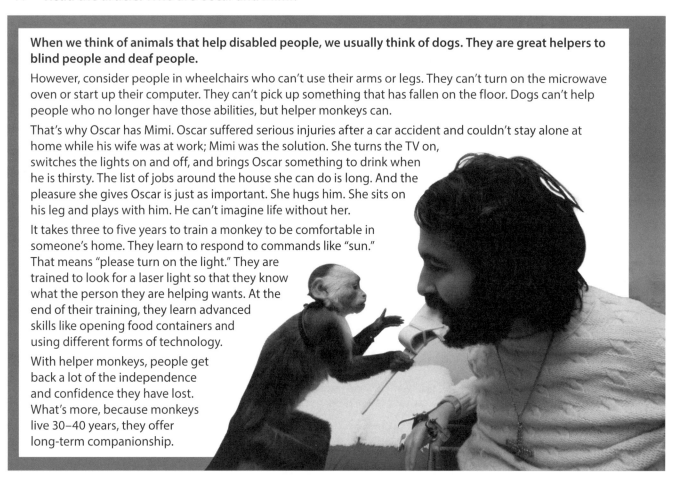

When we think of animals that help disabled people, we usually think of dogs. They are great helpers to blind people and deaf people.

However, consider people in wheelchairs who can't use their arms or legs. They can't turn on the microwave oven or start up their computer. They can't pick up something that has fallen on the floor. Dogs can't help people who no longer have those abilities, but helper monkeys can.

That's why Oscar has Mimi. Oscar suffered serious injuries after a car accident and couldn't stay alone at home while his wife was at work; Mimi was the solution. She turns the TV on, switches the lights on and off, and brings Oscar something to drink when he is thirsty. The list of jobs around the house she can do is long. And the pleasure she gives Oscar is just as important. She hugs him. She sits on his leg and plays with him. He can't imagine life without her.

It takes three to five years to train a monkey to be comfortable in someone's home. They learn to respond to commands like "sun." That means "please turn on the light." They are trained to look for a laser light so that they know what the person they are helping wants. At the end of their training, they learn advanced skills like opening food containers and using different forms of technology.

With helper monkeys, people get back a lot of the independence and confidence they have lost. What's more, because monkeys live 30–40 years, they offer long-term companionship.

B **RECALL KEY INFORMATION** Look at the questions. Can you remember the information? Check your answers in the article.

1 Why can't Oscar use his arms and legs?

2 What are two things Mimi does for Oscar?

3 How long is the monkey's training?

4 How long do monkeys live?

2 LISTENING

A 🔊 **9.01** Listen to part of a talk show. Check (✓) the topic the people discuss. Do you agree with Vince or with Carla? Why?

if people ever have trouble with their monkey helpers ☐

if monkey helpers get enough training ☐

if it is dangerous to have monkeys in people's home ☐

if it is right to use monkeys to help people ☐

3 WRITING

A Read the response to exercise 2A and circle the words that show the writer's attitude.

> I have to say that I completely agree with Carla here. It's obviously important to help the disabled be as independent as possible, but we're forcing these monkeys to lead unnatural lives. Sadly, this is the case with many service animals. Frankly, I think it's very unfair the animals.

B Do you agree or disagree with the use of service animals to help the disabled? Why? Use adverbs to show your attitude.

_____

_____

_____

_____

_____

_____

_____

_____

_____

CHECK AND REVIEW

Read the statements. Can you do these things?

UNIT 9	Mark the boxes. ✔ I can do it. ? I am not sure. I can …		If you are not sure, go back to these pages in the Student's Book.
VOCABULARY	☐	use nouns and compound nouns to name different places.	page 86
	☐	talk about rules.	page 88
GRAMMAR	☐	express prohibition, permission, and obligation in the present.	page 87 page 89
	☐	express prohibition, permission, and obligation in the past.	
FUNCTIONAL LANGUAGE	☐	use phrases to make generalizations.	page 90
	☐	give contrasting information.	page 91
SKILLS	☐	express opinions in writing.	page 93
	☐	use adverbs to show attitude.	page 93

1   VOCABULARY: Talking about discoveries

A   **Match 1–9 in column A with a–i in column B.**

A		B	
1	In their research, scientists noticed a ___f___	a	phenomenon of frog behavior before bad weather.
2	They have been investigating the _____	b	solution yet.
3	They have been trying to gain _____	c	important knowledge about predicting weather.
4	Scientists have faced _____	d	breakthrough in understanding animal behavior.
5	Studying frogs has provided _____	e	insights into how birds behave before storms.
6	Researchers believe they have made a _____	f	connection between weather and animal behavior.
7	Scientists have carried out _____	g	many challenges in doing this kind of research.
8	Nobody has been able to provide a _____	h	an important discovery in the future.
9	They are hoping to make _____	i	research into unusual animal behavior.

2   GRAMMAR: Past unreal conditionals

A   **Read the situations. Then choose the sentence that explains the situation.**

1   We went out to eat because there was no food in the fridge.

   a   We wouldn't have gone out to eat if there had been food in the fridge.

   b   There would have been food in the fridge if we had gone out to eat.

2   Sylvia didn't go to the party because she had to work late.

   a   If Sylvia had gone to the party, she wouldn't have had to work late.

   b   If Sylvia hadn't had to work late, she would have gone to the party.

3   The forest fire started because someone at a campsite was careless.

   a   If the forest fire hadn't started, someone at a campsite wouldn't have been careless.

   b   If someone at a campsite hadn't been careless, the forest fire wouldn't have started.

4   George lost the race because he started one second late.

   a   George wouldn't have lost the race if he hadn't started one second late.

   b   George wouldn't have started one second late if he hadn't lost the race.

B   **Put the words in the correct order to form sentences with unreal past conditionals.**

1   known / I / would / had / if / have / come / I
    I would have come if I had known. OR If I had known, I would have come.

2   them / you / helped / asked / if / boys / have / the / had / would
    _____

3   more careful / fallen / been / you / you / if / had / have / wouldn't
    _____

4   we / the / been / sick / gone on vacation / have / baby / hadn't / if / would
    _____

5   you / if / would / seen you / the doctor / an appointment / earlier / have / made / had
    _____

6   you / you / would / had / I / me / texted / have / if / told
    _____

3   GRAMMAR AND VOCABULARY

A   **Complete the sentences with the phrases in the box. Then rewrite the sentences with unreal past conditionals.**

| a breakthrough | challenges | a connection | ~~the phenomenon~~ | research | a solution |

1   Scientists didn't investigate _the phenomenon_ because they had no funding.
    Scientists would have investigated the phenomenon if they'd had funding. OR If scientists had had
    funding, they would have investigated the phenomenon.

2   Scientists didn't notice _____ between cars and climate change because they didn't have enough information.
    _____
    _____

3   Researchers made _____ because they performed new experiments.
    _____
    _____

4   Scientists carried out new _____ because they didn't understand the problem.
    _____
    _____

5   It took years to complete the research because the researchers faced so many _____ .
    _____
    _____

6   Scientists were able to provide _____ because their research was successful.
    _____
    _____

BIG MISTAKE!

1 VOCABULARY: Discussing right and wrong

A **Do these sentences mean the same thing? Write _S_ (same) or _D_ (different).**

1	It was an epic fail.	It was a small mistake.	D
2	You'll have to correct the error.	You'll have to correct the mistake.	S
3	He blames me.	He says it's my fault.	
4	It was a real blunder.	It was a big mistake.	
5	I'll fix the problem.	I'll make it right.	
6	There was confusion.	There was an error.	
7	I got it wrong.	I made it right.	
8	There was a mix-up.	There was a misunderstanding.	
9	They didn't get it right.	They made an error.	

2 GRAMMAR: Past modals

A **Complete the sentences. Use the words in parentheses ( ). Add _not_ where necessary.**

1 Why didn't you tell me you were hungry? I _____could have given_____ (could / give) you something to eat.

2 I wanted to go to the party, too. You _____ (should / go) without me.

3 It's too bad you didn't take any medicine. It _____ (might / help).

4 I'm sorry. I didn't know you needed money. I _____ (could / lend) you some.

5 I didn't know you had a problem. You _____ (should / call).

6 I told Charlie never to text and drive. He _____ (might / have) the accident if he'd listened to me.

7 David was supposed to meet me at the station but he didn't. He _____ (may / miss) his train.

8 Marta's computer was hacked. She _____ (should / change) her password more often.

B   **Write responses to the sentences in 1-8. Use *could, might,* and *should* and the words in the box.**

accept their job offer	fix it	get the position	have a good time
leave for work earlier	receive some gifts	walk	~~win~~

1 It's too bad you didn't run in the race.
   You might have won. OR You could have won.

2 Why didn't you apply for the job?
   _____

3 It's too bad Araceli didn't come to the party.
   _____

4 It was a mistake not to take the other job.
   _____

5 It's too bad Josh was late for work.
   _____

6 Why didn't you tell us it was your birthday?
   _____

7 Why did you take the bus?
   _____

8 Why did they blame me for the problem?
   _____

3 GRAMMAR AND VOCABULARY

A   **Complete the sentences with your own ideas.**

1 Maxine didn't correct the mistake until a month later.
   She should _____ have corrected it right away _____.

2 It wasn't your fault.
   You couldn't _____.

3 I couldn't fix the problem by myself. I should
   _____.

4 I thought Martin told you the meeting had been canceled.
   It was a mix-up.
   I should _____.

5 Kara was to blame for the accident.
   She shouldn't _____.

6 It was an epic fail.
   I might _____.

7 It was a mistake to invite only some of my co-workers to
   the party.
   I should _____.

8 There was a lot of confusion about where to meet.
   I should _____.

10.3 YOU'LL NEVER GUESS!

1 FUNCTIONAL LANGUAGE: Engaging listeners

A **Circle the correct words.**

1 You won't *believe / think* this, but our flight was canceled.

2 Well, you *can / do* imagine. We were really upset.

3 Yeah, but you know *how / what*? We ended up getting free plane tickets.

4 *Are you / Do you get* ready for this?

5 They upgraded us to first-class seats. *Is / Isn't* that amazing?

6 We went out to look for the dog, and *don't / wouldn't* you know it? He was in the backyard the whole time.

7 So I found $100 on my way to the interview. But that's not *it / all*! I got the job, too!

2 REAL-WORLD STRATEGY: Showing interest in a story

A **Complete the conversation with the expressions in the box.**

Let me guess – you	~~Don't tell me you~~	You must be joking.	That's so awful

A My boss is really angry at me.

B ¹ *Don't tell me you* were late for work again!

A Yup. That's the third time this month.

B ² _____ forgot to set your alarm clock.

A No, I set it. But the power went out in the middle of the night and reset it.

B ³ _____ . You have the worst luck.

A Yeah, tell me about it. Anyway, I tried to explain, but my boss said if it happens again he'd fire me.

B ⁴ _____ . What are you going to do?

A Get to work on time! What else can I do?

3 FUNCTIONAL LANGUAGE AND REAL-WORLD STRATEGY

A **Complete the conversation with the expressions from exercises 1A and 2A.**

Ari You're back from your vacation. You look great! How was the hotel where you stayed?

Dia We never got there. You'll never ¹ <u>guess what happened</u> .

Ari What?

Dia We rented a car at the airport. You won't ² _____, but twenty minutes after we left the airport, we got a flat tire.

Ari Seriously? A flat tire on a rented car?

Dia We weren't happy. You can imagine. Anyway, while we were trying to change the tire, a man from the island stopped and asked if we needed help. By the time he changed the tire, it was lunchtime, so he invited us to have lunch with his family.

Ari Don't ³ _____ you went to a stranger's home for lunch!'

Dia Everyone in the family was so friendly. They were happy to have us for lunch. Their home was next to the beach. ⁴ _____? They had an extra room, and we ended up staying there.

Ari You must ⁵ _____! The whole week?

Dia Yeah. The whole week. Isn't ⁶ _____? The funny thing is we didn't need the car at all. We never went anywhere else on the island.

B **Imagine you are Dia. Something else surprising happened during the vacation. Write the conversation with expressions from exercises 1A and 2A. Use an idea in the box or your own idea.**

> You took the wrong suitcase at the airport. A famous person was at the beach every day.
> Your flight home was canceled.

Dia <u>You'll never guess what else happened to me.</u> _____

Ari _____

Dia _____

Ari _____

Dia _____

Ari _____

Dia _____

Ari _____

10.4 I CAN'T LIVE WITHOUT IT!

1 LISTENING

A   🔊 **10.01** **Listen to a conversation. What things do the man and woman agree they could not live without?**

B   🔊 **10.02** **LISTEN FOR TONE** **Listen to the tone of the speakers' voices. Circle the correct answers.**

1 "You mean like air, food, and water?"
   (a) She is trying to be funny.
   b She wants information.

2 "Paper and pen?"
   a She is asking if he needs paper and a pen.
   b She is surprised.

3 "I just love them."
   a He is saying a fact.
   b He is not serious.

4 "Really, I couldn't live without either of my parents."
   a He is saying a fact.
   b He is trying to be funny.

5 "Sunsets at the beach?"
   a She is asking him to repeat the question.
   b She is surprised.

2 READING

A   **Read the story. What did Olivia learn about living without the things she had loved before?**

When Olivia Stanton lost her job, she seemed to have lost everything. First it was her apartment and all the things she couldn't take when she moved in with her sister. There was her piano, her furniture, and the books she loved. The only thing she kept with her the whole time was her laptop computer. Without the computer, she wouldn't have been able to look for a job or stay in touch with friends.

For the first few months, Olivia found it very hard to live without all of her things. But as time went on, she learned she actually enjoyed life more with less stuff. She started looking for other things she could live without. She got rid of her car and started walking more or taking the bus. She gave up her gym membership and started running in the park instead.

She also started a blog about her new stuff-free lifestyle. From that blog, she got an offer to write a book and a $10,000 advance. With the $10,000, Olivia has been able to re-establish her life. She moved out of her sister's house and got a new apartment – a smaller one that fits with her new lifestyle. She has no desire to get back all the things she had before. Aside from the laptop, she has found that the only things she can't live without are her friends and the opportunities she found online.

B   **Circle the correct answers.**

1 Olivia moved out of her apartment *(after)/ before* she lost her job.

2 Olivia got rid of most of her things *when she moved to her sister's / because she needed the money.*

3 Olivia found that without all of her things life got *better / worse.*

4 Olivia was able to get a new apartment because she got a *new job / an offer to write a book.*

WRITING

A **Read the post from Olivia's blog. Circle the words that show contrast and underline the words that show similarity.**

When I think about my old lifestyle, it really couldn't be more different from how I live now. My life was full of things. I mean, I owned a lot of stuff, but the things I owned didn't really make me happy. I had a nice car, but I was always worried it would get scratched or dented whenever I drove somewhere. Similarly, I had a lot of really nice clothes, but I worked so much to afford them that I never had time to wear the outfits I liked so much. Now, on the other hand, I have a lot fewer things. But the things I do own are things I truly enjoy, and I also have time to actually enjoy them now.

B **Write a comment about what is and is not important in your life. Use the words from exercise 3A to help you.**

CHECK AND REVIEW

Read the statements. Can you do these things?

UNIT 10	Mark the boxes. ☑ I can do it. ? I am not sure. I can …	If you are not sure, go back to these pages in the Student's Book.
VOCABULARY	☐ use verb + noun phrases to describe research, investigation, and discovery.	page 98
	☐ talk about right and wrong.	page 100
GRAMMAR	☐ use past unreal conditionals to discuss present outcomes.	page 99
	☐ use modals of past probability to suggest unreal alternative outcomes.	page 101
FUNCTIONAL LANGUAGE	☐ keep a listener engaged.	page 102
	☐ show interest in a story.	page 103
SKILLS	☐ write a comment on a blog post.	page 105
	☐ use words to show similarity and contrast in writing.	page 105

11.1 STUDENT STORIES

1 VOCABULARY: Talking about college education

A **Use the words in the box to complete the email from a college student in his first week.**

association	~~campus~~	degrees	dorm	facilities	faculty	freshmen
grades	majors	professors	semester	society	undergraduate	

Hi Sis!

I just wanted to write quickly and let you know how things are going here. So far, everything's great! The
¹ _campus_ is really beautiful, but it's also huge. I've gotten lost a couple times. The ² _____ I'm
staying in is nice and modern, and my roommate seems like a nice guy. I think we'll get along really well. There was a meeting
for all the ³ _____ last night. It was a good chance to meet people since we're all new here. A couple members
of the ⁴ _____ were there also, although I won't meet any of my ⁵ _____ until classes start on
Monday.

The ⁶ _____ here are fantastic! The cafeteria is big and has
great food. There's a gym and a swimming pool…. There's even a library just for
⁷ _____ students. People studying for advanced ⁸ _____
apparently have a separate library.

I think I'm going to have a lot of fun this ⁹ _____ . I've already joined an
acting ¹⁰ _____ . But don't worry, I'm not going to neglect my studies or let
my ¹¹ _____ fall. I've also joined an
¹² _____ for engineering ¹³ _____ , so I'll have plenty of
study partners.

Anyway, gonna go now. Miss you lots,

Roberto

2 GRAMMAR: Gerund and infinitive after *forget*, *remember*, *stop*

A **Check (✓) the correct sentences. Then correct the mistakes in the incorrect sentences.**

1 I'll never forget climbing that
mountain. It was so exciting. ☑

2 Do you remember ~~to see~~ my
seeing
phone anywhere? ☐

3 You forgot texting me again.
Why can't you remember? ☐

4 I stopped buying some milk. Here it is. ☐

5 I stopped playing video games a few

years ago. I was playing them too much. ☐

6 Sorry. I didn't remember bringing
your book. I'll bring it tomorrow. ☐

7 I remember meeting the owner
of the business, but I can't remember
his name. ☐

8 I stopped at the ATM machine to
get some money. ☐

B **Complete the conversations. Use the words in parentheses ( ).**

1 **A** I can't find my phone.

   B I ___remember seeing___ (remember / see) you with it a short time ago.

2 **A** I didn't tell Anita and Diego about the party.

   B I'll _____ (remember / tell) them later on.

3 **A** I'm going out now.

   B Don't _____ (forget / get) something for dinner.

4 **A** What is something you will never forget?

   B I'll never _____ (forget / meet) my wife for the first time.

5 **A** Are these flowers for me?

   B Yes, I _____ (stopped / buy) them for you on my way
        home from work.

6 **A** Are you a vegetarian?

   B Yes, I _____ (stopped / eat) meat when I was in high school.

3 GRAMMAR AND VOCABULARY

A **Complete the conversations using the words in the box and the words in parentheses ( ).**

> campus   dorm   facilities   grades   professor   semester   society

1 **A** Thank goodness! My _____ are finally improving.

   B That's great. What are you doing differently?

   A I _____ (stop, play) so many video games.

2 **A** Did you finish your research paper?

   B What paper? I _____ (not, remember, have) a paper due this week!

   A Well, we have one. The _____ assigned it a month ago.

3 **A** So are you joining the theater _____ ?

   B No. I _____
        (forgot, sign up) by the deadline.

   A That's too bad. Well maybe you can join next
        _____ .

4 **A** Well, I'm back from my tour of the college.

   B Did you _____
        (remember, ask) about the gym and the
        swimming pool?

   A Yeah, we saw them. They're really nice
        _____ .

5 **A** Did you live in a _____
        in college?

   B At first. But I had the messiest roommate. He
        never cleaned up. I couldn't take it. I had to
        _____ (stop, live)
        with him and move into an apartment just
        off _____ .

FOLK REMEDIES

1 VOCABULARY: Talking about science

A Complete the sentences with the correct words in the box.

> science   scientist   scientific   ~~scientifically-proven~~

1 Something that is _____scientifically-proven_____ has been studied for a long time.
2 Chemistry is my favorite type of _____ .
3 Chris likes to read books about _____ subjects.
4 Have you always wanted to be a _____ ?

> research (n.)   researcher   research (v.)   research-based

5 _____ studies can take many years to complete.
6 _____ shows that sleep is necessary.
7 The _____ talked about the results of her study.
8 We have to _____ how to solve the problem.

> proof   prove   proven   scientifically-proven

9 Ginger is a _____ remedy for an upset stomach. Research has been done about it.
10 You have to _____ your ideas.
11 What _____ do you have?
12 This is a _____ fact.

> base (n.)   basis   base (v.)   based   scientifically-based

13 The report is _____ on research from three different universities.
14 What is the _____ of the study?
15 Students need a good _____ in mathematics.
16 You should _____ your research on children between the ages of 8 and 14.
17 All of the information is _____ . The research took place over 10 years.

> medicine   medical   medically-approved

18 The _____ exercises are helping my back pain. I should thank my doctor for showing them to me.
19 Do you like looking at _____ websites?
20 My cousin is majoring in _____ . She wants to be a doctor.

2 GRAMMAR: *help, let, make*

A **Circle the correct words. Sometimes more than one word is correct.**

1 We have a really furry dog, so we don't *help* / *(let)* / *make* him sit on the couch.

2 Warm milk *helps* / *lets* / *makes* me sleep.

3 Some kinds of music *help* / *let* / *make* me want to dance.

4 Snakes *help* / *let* / *make* a lot of people feel frightened.

5 Interesting activities *help* / *let* / *make* students learn.

6 Please be quiet and *help* / *let* / *make* the teacher speak.

B **Complete the sentences. Use *help, let*, or *make* and the correct pronoun.**

1 **A** Does your mother ever feel sleepy when she watches TV?

   B Yes, watching TV ____makes her____ feel sleepy.

2 **A** Why do you listen to that loud music?

   B It _____ relax.

3 **A** Do you stay out late at night?

   B Yes, my parents _____ stay out late.

4 **A** Did you have to do a lot of chores as a child?

   B Of course. Our parents _____ clean the house every Saturday.

5 **A** Can you please turn off the computer?

   B It won't _____ shut it down. It must be broken.

3 GRAMMAR AND VOCABULARY

A **Answer the questions. Try to use the words from exercise 1A in your answers.**

1 What's something that helps scientists conduct research?

_____

2 What can doctors do to make people trust them more?

_____

3 Should we let people take medicines that aren't medically-approved?

_____

4 What is a popular belief that is not scientifically-based?

_____

11.3 CAN YOU SUGGEST AN ALTERNATIVE?

1 FUNCTIONAL LANGUAGE: Discussing alternatives

A Complete the conversation. Use the words from the box.

also	alternative	another	~~can~~	else	great
is	like	might	that	work	

Customer Hello. I'm looking for a book for my 12-year-old nephew.

Bookseller This book has always worked well with boys of that age.

Customer ¹_____Can_____ you suggest an alternative? My nephew doesn't like sports very much.

Bookseller You could ²_____ try this book. It's very popular with boys and girls.

Customer It ³_____ not be the best option. He could think it's for girls. ⁴_____ there something different?

Bookseller Don't worry. We have plenty of books for that age group. ⁵_____ option would be this book about famous people in history.

Customer That could ⁶_____. Do you have anything ⁷_____?

Bookseller I also have these books on the animal world. They're a good ⁸_____.

Customer Hmm. I don't think they're a ⁹_____ choice. He's never shown an interest in animals.

Bookseller Then how about these comic books? They're very interesting. Boys love them.

Customer That looks ¹⁰_____ a good alternative.

Bookseller I also have these funny novels. They make kids laugh a lot.

Customer I like ¹¹_____ option, too. Now I have to decide which is better. It's not an easy choice!

2 REAL-WORLD STRATEGY: Giving a personal recommendation

A Complete the conversations with personal recommendations. Use your own ideas.

1 A I've been trying to lose weight but nothing seems to work. What would you suggest?

   B _____ has always worked for me.

2 A I'm thinking of buying a new car. What do you think I should get?

   B If I were you, _____.

3 A I spilled pasta sauce all over this shirt. What should I use to get the stain out?

   B I've always had good luck with _____.

4 A I have some vacation time coming up. Where do you think I should go?

   B _____

5 A It's my wife's birthday next week. Where do you think I should take her for dinner?

   B _____

3 FUNCTIONAL LANGUAGE AND REAL-WORLD STRATEGY

A **Nicolas is in a jewelry store talking to Carla, the store owner. Follow the instructions in parentheses ( ) to complete the conversation. Use the expressions in exercises 1A and 2A.**

Nicolas I'm looking for a gift for my girlfriend.

(Carla recommends a bracelet.)

Carla ¹ _____ If I were you, I'd choose a bracelet. _____ How about one of these?

(Nicolas likes that suggestion. Then he asks for options.)

Nicolas ² _____ But I was looking for something more elegant. ³ _____

(Carla suggests earrings as an alternative.)

Carla We have some beautiful necklaces. ⁴ _____

(Nicolas discusses the disadvantage of earrings.)

Nicolas ⁵ _____ My girlfriend doesn't wear earrings very often.

(Carla suggests the option of a matching bracelet and necklace.)

Carla ⁶ _____

(Nicolas responds to the suggestion.)

Nicolas ⁷ _____

(Carla recommends another bracelet and necklace.)

Carla ⁸ _____ The bracelet and necklace can be worn separately, or the bracelet can be attached to the necklace to make it longer. That way you have two necklaces.

(Nicolas likes that option.)

Nicolas ⁹ _____ I'll take it.

11.4 DRIVERLESS CARS? NO WAY!

1 READING

A **Read the article. Is the writer for or against driverless cars?**

People rarely like change. They find it frightening. Technology introduces something new, and people say they don't want it or need it.

How do you feel about riding in an elevator? You are probably comfortable. Can you imagine people ever being against an elevator? That is exactly what happened when elevators first appeared. At first, it was someone's job to operate the elevator. People on the elevator just had to get used to going up and down. But when elevators became automatic, people did not like the change at all. There was no human in control. People were scared to let a machine do everything.

So what happened? People got used to elevators. A soft voice gave instructions. There was relaxing music to calm the riders. Now it has been more than 150 years since the invention of the elevator, and people are against another invention: the driverless car. I hear my friends saying things like, "How will I be in control? The car will do anything it wants!"

The fact is that driverless cars will probably be safer than cars driven by human beings. People sometimes fall asleep at the wheel. They get distracted by their phones or by other passengers. And some people are just not very good drivers. With a driverless car, all of these problems disappear.

In the end, I predict the driverless car will become just like the elevator. People will be just as comfortable in a driverless car as they are in an elevator that is moving them from the first to the twenty-first floor.

B **IDENTIFYING ARGUMENTS** **Read the article again. Check (✓) the arguments the writer uses to support her opinion.**

1 New technology is frightening. ☐

2 People did not like elevators but eventually got used to them. ☐

3 Driverless cars are unsafe for small children and the elderly. ☐

3 People are already unsafe drivers, and driverless cars will be safer. ☐

4 Driverless cars will be much more comfortable than driving ourselves. ☐

2 LISTENING

A 🔊 **11.01** **Listen to the conversation. Write *T* (true) or *F* (false).**

1 The woman wants a driverless car. _____

2 The man will never want a driverless car. _____

3 The man likes to drive. _____

4 The woman doesn't think driverless cars are safer. _____

A   **Read the comment in response to the article. Circle the transition phrase that starts an opinion. Underline the transition phrases that add to the opinion. Draw a box around the transition phrase that ends the opinion.**

> ● ● ● ◁ ▷   🔍 🏠
>
> I'm not a car lover. I drive only because I have to. That doesn't mean I love the idea of driverless cars.
>
> First of all, driverless cars are really just computers on wheels. Computers are hacked all the time. What will prevent a hacker somewhere in the world from getting control of my car? More importantly, what will stop other people from making my car do dangerous things? It's also important to remember that driverless cars are programmed to drive on the road. What if there is an emergency and I need to drive off the road, perhaps into a field? Additionally, human drivers know that when they see a plastic bag on the road, it is not dangerous. A driverless car might not know that and might try to avoid it. That could cause an accident. Finally, think of all the people who will lose their jobs if drivers are no longer needed. What will happen to them?

B   **Write a response to the article in exercise 1A. Give your opinion about driverless cars. Use the correct transition phrases.**

_____

_____

_____

_____

_____

CHECK AND REVIEW

Read the statements. Can you do these things?

UNIT 11	Mark the boxes. ☑ I can do it. ? I am not sure. I can …		If you are not sure, go back to these pages in the Student's Book.
VOCABULARY	☐	use words to talk about college life.	page 108
	☐	use different word forms to discuss science and medicine.	page 110
GRAMMAR	☐	change meaning by using gerunds or infinitives after *forget*, *remember*, and *stop*.	page 109
	☐	use causative verbs *help*, *let*, and *make* to indicate effects caused by someone or something else.	page 111
FUNCTIONAL LANGUAGE	☐	discuss alternatives.	page 112
	☐	give a personal recommendation.	page 113
SKILLS	☐	write a comment in response to an article.	page 115
	☐	use transition phrases to add to and conclude arguments.	page 115

12.1 PHOTO STORIES

1 VOCABULARY: Talking about the senses

A **Match the descriptions in column A with the adjectives in column B.**

A		B	
	A		**B**
1	the way a piece of cake should taste _e_	**a**	bright
2	the way a baby's cheek feels	**b**	colorful
3	the way a song can sound	**c**	damp
4	the way old books can smell	**d**	deep
5	the way a man's voice can sound	**e**	flavorful
6	the way a small child's voice can sound	**f**	fresh
7	a day when the sun is shining	**g**	high-pitched
8	the way a wet towel can smell	**h**	melodic
9	the way the skin of a lemon feels	**i**	musty
10	the way grass can smell after it rains	**j**	rough
11	a shirt that is orange, yellow, green, and blue	**k**	smooth

B **Write sentences about what you like and don't like. Use the adjectives in exercise 1A and the nouns in the box, or your own ideas.**

clothes	faces	fish	fruit		meals	music	rooms
soap	socks	sounds	summer days		~~voices~~	weather	wool

1 In my opinion, long beards are a fad. I don't think they'll be popular next year.
2
3
4
5
6

2 GRAMMAR: Adding emphasis

A **Check (✓) the sentences that add emphasis to an idea. Then underline the words that add emphasis.**

1 <u>What I do in my free time</u> is not your concern. ☑
2 The thing I like most about my job is the money. ☐
3 What do you remember most about elementary school? ☐
4 The thing I love about my home is the light. ☐
5 What I don't want is another problem with my car. ☐
6 What do you mean when you say you don't understand? ☐

B **Complete the sentences. Use the words in parentheses ( ). Write two sentences with your own ideas.**

1 The _____thing I like most about Florida is_____ the weather. (I like most about Florida)
2 What _____ the noise. (bothers me a lot)
3 What _____ a vacation. (I need)
4 What _____ her name. (I can never remember)
5 What _____ my children's health. (worries me all the time)
6 The _____ saying goodbye. (I hate the most)
7 What _____ science fiction novels. (I really like to read)
8 The _____ .
9 What _____ .

3 GRAMMAR AND VOCABULARY

A **Answer the questions. Add emphasis to your ideas. Try to use the words from exercise 2B in your responses.**

1 What was the thing you most liked to eat when you were a child?
   The thing I most liked to eat was a banana.

2 What do you like the most about your home?
   _____

3 What do you want most of all in the future?
   _____

4 What is something you love doing on the weekend?
   _____

5 What do you dislike the most about your town?
   _____

6 What is the thing you enjoy the most on social media?
   _____

12.2 DID THAT REALLY HAPPEN?

1 VOCABULARY: Describing memories

A **Write the word that matches the definition.**

bring back	childhood	~~clear~~	distant	early
long-term	look back on	recall	recent	recognize
remind someone of	short-term	vague	vivid	

1 describing memories that are easy to see in your mind — _clear_

2 describing memories or events that happened a short time ago _____

3 describing memories that stay in your mind for a lot of time _____

4 describing memories that produce strong images in your mind _____

5 describing memories that are temporary _____

6 describing memories or events that happened a long time ago _____

7 describing memories that are not complete or uncertain _____

8 the part of your life when you were young _____

9 describing some of the first memories you have _____

10 to know people or places because you have seen or experienced them before _____

11 to think about a time in your past _____

12 to make someone think of someone or something else _____

13 to remember a fact or event _____

14 to make someone think about something from the past _____

B **Complete the sentences with words from exercise 1A. Don't use the same word twice. Then rewrite the sentences so that they are true for you.**

1 The thing I _____recall_____ most about my childhood is my family's farm.

The thing I recall most about my childhood is playing with my brother and sister.

2 When I _____ my childhood, I get sad.

_____

_____

3 Going back to my old neighborhood _____ me of the past.

_____

_____

4 I have very _____ memories of my grandparents. It's like they are still here with me.

_____

_____

5 Getting together with all my cousins _____ wonderful memories.

_____

_____

6 I have a _____ memory of my first school. I remember the outside but not the classrooms.

_____

_____

GRAMMAR: Substitution and referencing

A   **Complete the sentences. Use the words in the boxes.**

~~it~~   one   ones   them

1   If we don't have your email address, please send ___it___ .
2   If these videos don't interest you, tell us the _____ you would like to see.
3   If you don't have a teacher, we will find you _____ .
4   I got you these books. I hope you like _____ .

did   do   not   so

5   Do you want to learn more? If _____ , please write us today.
6   I didn't learn anything, but other people _____ .
7   Are you going to do the required work? If _____ , we can't help you.
8   I don't have a lot of free time, but they _____ .

B   **Underline the words that are repeated. Then replace the underlined words.**

1   If you don't remember the number, I can give <u>the number</u> *it* to you.
2   Do you want to improve your memory? If you want to improve your memory, read this.
3   My brother doesn't remember our childhood well, but I remember.
4   I played with my cousins on Sundays. I got together with my cousins at my grandparents' home.
5   I don't recall a pink house, but I remember a green house.
6   Does Hilda remember? If Hilda doesn't remember, ask Nick.

C   **Look at the sentences with substitutions or referents. Write the sentences that come before them. Use your own ideas.**

1   _____*Are you going to do the dishes?*_____ If not, I'll do them.
2   _____ I have brown ones.
3   _____ , but I did. I went often.
4   _____ I felt bad because I was the only
one who didn't.
5   _____ , but I do.
6   _____ If so, let me know.

1 FUNCTIONAL LANGUAGE: Recalling past experiences

A **Correct five mistakes in the conversation.**

Natalia I love this picture.

Greg Where was that taken?

Natalia Don't ~~say to~~ *tell* me you don't remember the high school picnic.

Greg Which picnic?

Natalia The picnic when it started to rain.

Greg Oh yeah. That rings. We all ran under a tree. That was really dumb.

Natalia Well, are you remembering the time it started to rain at the soccer game?

Greg No. I didn't recall rain at a soccer game. Are you sure I was there?

Natalia Absolutely. You were the only one who had an umbrella. We all tried to get under it.

Greg Yeah. It all comes back to me now. That was funny!

2 REAL-WORLD STRATEGY: Sharing experiences

A **Complete the conversation. Use the phrases in the box.**

had a similar experience	of a story	that ever happened	that's like the time

Luis Once I was fishing. I took off my watch and it fell in the lake. That was the end of that watch! Has ¹_____ to you?

Renée Well, I haven't lost anything in a lake, but that reminds me ²_____ . ³_____ that I lost my glasses. I'd put them on the top of the car. I started driving. Then I realized I wasn't wearing my glasses. When I got out of the car, they weren't there anymore.

Joel You know, I ⁴_____ once, but in my case I had left my house keys on top of the car. When I got home, I had to break the window to get into the house.

3 FUNCTIONAL LANGUAGE AND REAL-WORLD STRATEGY

A **Read the stories. Then complete the conversation. Use the facts in the stories and your own ideas.**

> Amanda and Ron took a bike trip with other friends a few years ago. One day they were in a village. A dog ran across the road right in front of Amanda. She tried to avoid hitting the dog and fell off the bike. She couldn't get up because she was in a lot of pain. Some villagers came to help her. One of them took her to the local hospital. Her friends rode their bikes there. It was a very small hospital. It turned out she had broken her arm and couldn't continue on the bike trip.

> Manuel once fell off a horse when he was on vacation. He'd been riding the horse when something scared it. The horse threw Manuel off and ran away. At first, Manuel's shoulder hurt him, but he was OK. He was able to walk and found the horse about a mile down the road.

Amanda   Do you remember that time _____ *I broke my arm on the bike trip?*

Ron   That trip's a bit vague for me. _____

_____

Amanda   Don't tell me you don't remember, Ron. _____

_____

Ron   Oh yeah, that rings a bell. _____
Amanda   _____

_____

Ron   Yeah, it's all coming back to me now. _____

_____ Has that ever happened to you, Manuel?

Manuel   That reminds me of a story, but not with a bike. That's like the time that _____

_____

Ron   You know, I had a similar experience once with a horse. _____

_____

12.4 MAN'S BEST FRIEND?

1 LISTENING

A 🔊 **12.01** **Listen to the conversation. Answer the questions.**

1 Who are Lily and Chelsea?

2 What does the woman dislike about Dan's dog?

3 According to Dan, how does the dog show happiness?

4 According to Vic, what does Dan do that is dangerous?

B 🔊 **12.01** **LISTEN FOR EXAMPLES** **Listen again. Put the words and phrases from the conversation in the order that you hear them. Then check (✓) whether they are transitions to change from one topic to another or examples to support an argument.**

		Transition	Example
_____	The thing is	☐	☐
_____	like (jumping)	☐	☐
_____	In fact	☐	☐
_____	I mean … just think about	☐	☐
_____	For instance	☐	☐
1	Actually	☑	☐

2 READING

A **Read advice for training a dog. Then choose the best title for each piece of advice.**

| Dog training | Contact us | Reviews |

There's nothing a dog likes more than food. When you're training your dog, always have something in your pocket to reward the dog's good behavior. This way the dog will repeat the behavior. It's like you and your paycheck. You wouldn't go to work if you didn't get one. The treat your dog gets is like a paycheck. It makes the dog want to continue going "to work."

When you're in a public space, it's important to control your dog. That's why the dog must be trained not to leave your side. Start the training in your home. Dogs are usually taught to stay to the left, but it's OK if you prefer the right. When you give the dog a treat for good behavior, make sure it's from the hand next to the dog. You don't want it to go in front of you to get the treat. When the dog has gotten good in your home at not moving from your side, the dog is ready to continue its training outside.

a Make your dog want to come when you call

b Teach your dog to walk beside you

c Train your dog with something it loves

d Train your dog not to touch dangerous things

3 WRITING

A   Read a summary of an opinion about dog training classes. Underline contrasting ideas. Circle the words that link them.

> The speaker argued that dog training classes should not be required. She claimed that many dogs still misbehave despite having had training. She argued that some types of dogs are just naturally more obedient, and that other types of dogs naturally resist training. Personally, I disagree. While it is true that some dogs are more naturally obedient, all dogs benefit from training, and there's not a dog that can't be trained with enough work.

B   🔊 **12.01** Listen again. Take notes on Vic's and Dan's arguments. Write a summary contrasting their opinions. Mention the points that you agree and disagree with. Conclude your summary with a general opinion.

_____
_____
_____
_____
_____
_____
_____
_____

CHECK AND REVIEW

Read the statements. Can you do these things?

UNIT 12	Mark the boxes. ✔ I can do it. ? I am not sure. I can ...	If you are not sure, go back to these pages in the Student's Book.
VOCABULARY	☐ use sense adjectives for descriptions.	page 118
	☐ use words to describe and share memories.	page 120
GRAMMAR	☐ emphasize something by using the structure *What I remember most is ...* or *The thing I liked was ...* .	page 119
	☐ use substitution and referencing to avoid repetition.	page 121
FUNCTIONAL LANGUAGE	☐ recall a memory.	page 122
	☐ share experiences.	page 123
SKILLS	☐ write a summary of an opinion.	page 125
	☐ write about contrasting ideas.	page 125

1.5 TIME TO SPEAK Job interviews

A **Which of the following do you think are common interview questions in your country? Write two more interview questions. Why do you think companies ask these questions?**

Where do you see yourself in five years? ☐

Are you married? ☐

What is your greatest weakness? ☐

How much did you make in your last job? ☐

_____

_____

B **How would you answer the questions you checked in exercise A? Write your answers.**

2.5 TIME TO SPEAK Restaurant rescue

A **Think of a restaurant you don't like in your town. Make a list of the things you don't like about it.**

_____   _____

_____   _____

_____   _____

B **Write a letter to the owner offering suggestions on how he/she can improve the restaurant.**

3.5 TIME TO SPEAK A whole new lifestyle

A **Read the beginning of the story below. Complete the story with an expected change in Erika's lifestyle. Go online and find three pictures to help tell the story.**

In college, Erika wanted to travel the world. But a year after Erika just graduated college, she was still living with her parents. She hadn't found a job yet, and she certainly didn't have money to travel. This was _not_ how she had planned her life. So she decided to …

B **Share the photos in the next class. Can anyone guess your story?**

4.5 TIME TO SPEAK Design an ad

A **Look online for an ad written in English. Write a description of the ad.**

- What product is it selling?
- Where does the ad appear? On television? On a website? On a billboard?
- What advertising techniques does it use?
- Do you think the ad is effective? Why or why not?

B **Describe the ad in your next class. Are your classmates familiar with the ad? Do they agree with your opinion of the ad?**

5.5 TIME TO SPEAK A chance meeting

A   **Look back at the story on page 52 of the Student's Book. Then answer the questions.**
- What happens in the story?
- What kind of story is it?

B   **Choose one of the story types below. Change the details of the story on page 52 of the Student's Book to fit the new story type.**
- coming-of-age story
- mystery
- success story
- tear jerker

C   **Present your new story at the next class. Can your classmates guess the new story type?**

6.5 TIME TO SPEAK Your urban art project

A   **Go online and find an urban art project somewhere in the world that you think is interesting.**
- What is the project?
- Where is it?
- Who is involved in the project?
- What are the goals of the project?

B   **Write a report about the project and bring it to the next class. Explain it and discuss it with the rest of the class.**

7.5 TIME TO SPEAK Online communication survey

A   **Choose one of the online activities below or think of a different online activity.**
- online dating
- online shopping
- online gaming
- watching online videos
- listening to podcasts

B   **Create a survey about the activity you chose. Think of four or five questions to ask about it. Give the survey to your family and friends or post it on one of your social media accounts.**

C   **Bring the results to your next class. Explain your survey and present the results to the rest of the class.**

EXTRA ACTIVITIES

8.5 TIME TO SPEAK Planning a digital detox

A   Try a digital detox between now and your next class. What online activities are you willing to give up?

- ☐ checking your social media accounts
- ☐ reading articles online
- ☐ watching videos online
- ☐ texting/messaging friends and family
- ☐ using apps on your phone

B   Make a digital detox plan to help you give up the activities you checked in A.

C   In your next class describe your plan for a digital detox and report back to the class. Where you successful? Why or why not?

9.5 TIME TO SPEAK Sell it!

A   Go online and research a technology, device, or service that helps people with a disability.

- ■ What is the technology, device, or service?
- ■ What type of disability is it for?
- ■ How does it help a disabled person?
- ■ Who pays for it? (the disabled person, the government, a charity, …)

B   Write a summary of the technology, device, or service you researched.

C   Bring the summary to your next class. Explain the technology, device, or service to the class.

10.5 TIME TO SPEAK Turning points

A   Think of the kinds of events that can change people's lives completely (a turning point). Think of a friend or family member who has had an interesting turning point in his/her life. Make a video asking the person about the turning point, or go online and find someone talking about a turning point in his/her life.

B   Bring the video to your next class. Explain how the person's life would be different if the turning point had not happened.

11.5 TIME TO SPEAK Mediation

A   Think of a time you mediated a disagreement between co-workers or friends.

- ■ What was the disagreement about?
- ■ What solution did you suggest?
- ■ Were both people happy with the solution you suggested? Why or why not?

B   In your next class, describe the disagreement and the solution you suggested.

12.5 TIME TO SPEAK Where were you when …?

A   **Choose one of the events below that you remember, or go online and choose a different historic event that has occurred in your lifetime.**

- June 22, 1986 – Diego Maradona's "Hand of God" goal
- November 10, 1989 – the fall of the Berlin wall
- April 5, 1994 – the death of Kurt Cobain
- December 31, 2000 – the world prepared for Y2K … and nothing happened
- December 5, 2013 – the death of Nelson Mandela

B   **Make notes about what you remember most about the event you chose.**

C   **In your next class, describe the event and what you remember about it. Do your classmates remember the event as well? Do their memories match yours?**

The authors and publishers acknowledge the following sources of copyright material and are grateful for the permissions granted. While every effort has been made, it has not always been possible to identify the sources of all the material used, or to trace all copyright holders. If any omissions are brought to our notice, we will be happy to include the appropriate acknowledgements on reprinting and in the next update to the digital edition, as applicable.

Photographs

Key: B = Below, BL = Below Left, BR = Below Right, C = Centre, CL = Centre Left, CR = Centre Right, TC = Top Centre, TL = Top Left, TR = Top Right.

All the photographs are sourced from Getty Images.

p. 2 , p. 53: Hero Images; p. 3: Boris Breuer/The Image Bank; p. 4: maroke/iStock/Getty Images Plus; p. 5: shironosov/iStock/Getty Images Plus; p. 7, p. 55: Jose Luis Pelaez Inc/Blend Images; p. 10: Tony C French/The Image Bank; p. 11: foxestacado/iStock/Getty Images Plus; p. 12: Eisenhut and Mayer Wien/Photolibrary; p. 13: Alain Schroeder/ONOKY; p. 14: XiXinXing; p. 15: altrendo images/Altrendo; p. 16: petekarici/E+; p. 18: JGI/Blend Images; p. 19: SKA/Cultura Exclusive; p. 20: dardespot/E+; p. 21: Jon Feingersh/Blend Images; p. 22 (TR): Kwangmoozaa/iStock/Getty Images Plus; p. 22 (BL): Asia Images Group; p. 23: Yagi-Studio/E+; p. 24: vinhdav/iStock Editorial/Getty Images Plus; p. 26: AfricaImages/iStock/Getty Images Plus; p. 27: Stewart Bremner/Moment; p. 29: Benjamin Torode/Moment; p. 30: Yellow Dog Productions/The Image Bank; p. 31: SolisImages/iStock/Getty Images Plus; p. 32 (TR): PhotoAlto/Milena Boniek/Brand X Pictures; p. 32 (CR): Mauro-Matacchione/iStock/Getty Images Plus; p. 34: kzenon/iStock/Getty Images Plus; p. 35: LWA/The Image Bank; p. 37: AntonioGuillem/iStock/Getty Images Plus; p. 38: martin-dm/E+; p. 39: BakiBG/iStock/Getty Images Plus; p. 40: tommaso79/iStock/Getty Images Plus; p. 42: Blend Images - KidStock/Brand X Pictures; p. 43, p. 51: Tetra Images; p. 44: fstop123/iStock/Getty Images Plus; p. 45: Mauro-Matacchione/iStock/Getty Images Plus; p. 46: Maskot; p. 47 (TL): ElenaNichizhenova/iStock/Getty Images Plus; p. 47 (CL): Mikael Vaisanen/Corbis; p. 47 (TR): HASLOO/iStock/Getty Images Plus; p. 47 (CR): Jupiterimages/Photolibrary; p. 48: Johner Images; p. 50: Zero Creatives/Cultura; p. 52: PeopleImages/E+; p. 54: Phil Boorman/Cultura; p. 56: photosoup/iStock/Getty Images Plus; p. 59: Tara Moore/Taxi; p. 60: Image Source/Seb Oliver; p. 61: Igor Ustynskyy/Moment; p. 62: ImagesBazaar; p. 63: yanyong/iStock/Getty Images Plus; p. 64: levente bodo/Moment; p. 66 (TL): Joe_Potato/iStock/Getty Images Plus; p. 66 (TR): WIN-Initiative; p. 66 (TC): Alan Schein Photography/Corbis; p. 66 (CL): Comstock/Stockbyte; p. 66 (TR): Andrey Rudakov/Bloomberg; p. 66 (C): Teddy Morduhovich/EyeEm; p. 66 (BL): Wayne Eastep/Photographer's Choice; p. 66 (BC): YOSHIHIRO TAKADA/a.collectionRF; p. 66 (BR): Caiaimage/Sam Edwards; p. 67: Creatas/Getty Images Plus; p. 68: Photograph by Bernd Zillich/Moment; p. 69: Mike Powell/Allsport Concepts; p. 70: stsvirkun/iStock/Getty Images Plus; p. 71 (TR): Tom Merton/Caiaimage; p. 71 (B), p. 83: Ariel Skelley/DigitalVision; p. 72: Bettmann; p. 74: undefined undefined/iStock/Getty Images Plus; p. 75, p. 95: Westend61; p. 76: bowdenimages/iStock/Getty Images Plus; p. 77: Mario Castello/Corbis; p. 78: aapskyiStock/Getty Images Plus; p. 79: Bobex-73/iStock/Getty Images Plus; p. 80: SergioProvilskyi/iStock/Getty Images Plus; p. 82: Fuse/Corbis; p. 85: Juzant/DigitalVision; p. 86: Portra Images/DigitalVision; p. 87: pawel.gaul/E+; p. 88: Hulton Archive; p. 91: typhoonski/iStock/Getty Images Plus; p. 92: Roetting+Pollex/LOOK; p. 94: Denis Torkhov/iStock/Getty Images Plus; p. 96: Kane Skennar/DigitalVision.

Front cover photography by Alija/E+.

Audio production by CityVox, New York.

Corpus

Development of this publication has made use of the Cambridge English Corpus (CEC). The CEC is a multi-billion word collection of contemporary spoken and written English. It includes British English, American English, and other varieties. It also includes the Cambridge Learner Corpus, the world's biggest collection of learner writing, developed in collaboration with Cambridge Assessment. Cambridge University Press uses the CEC to provide evidence about language use that helps to produce better language teaching materials. Our Evolve authors study the Corpus to see how English is really used, and to identify typical learner mistakes. This information informs the authors' selection of vocabulary, grammar items and Student's Book Corpus features such as the Accuracy Check, Register Check, and Insider English.